W9-DCC-096

DEVELOPING CASEWORK SKILLS

SAGE HUMAN SERVICES GUIDES, VOLUME 15

SAGE HUMAN SERVICES GUIDES

a series of books edited by ARMAND LAUFFER

Volume 1: **GRANTSMANSHIP**
by Armand Lauffer with contributions by Milan Dluhy,
William Lawrence, and Eloise Snyder

Volume 2: **CREATING GROUPS**
by Harvey J. Bertcher and Frank F. Maple

Volume 3: **UNDERSTANDING YOUR SOCIAL AGENCY**
by Armand Lauffer, Lynn Nybell, Carla Overberger,
Beth Reed, and Lawrence Zeff

Volume 4: **SHARED DECISION MAKING**
by Frank F. Maple

Volume 5: **VOLUNTEERS**
by Armand Lauffer and Sarah Gorodezky with
contributions by Jay Callahan and Carla Overberger

Volume 6: **RESOURCES: For Child Placement and Other Human Services**
by Armand Lauffer with contributions by Bonnie Carlson,
Kayla Conrad, and Lynn Nybell

Volume 7: **FINDING FAMILIES: An Ecological Approach to Family Assessment
in Adoption**
by Ann Hartman

Volume 8: **NO CHILD IS UNADOPTABLE: A Reader on Adoption of
Children with Special Needs**
by Sallie R. Churchill, Bonnie Carlson, and Lynn Nybell

Volume 9: **HEALTH NEEDS OF CHILDREN**
by Roger Manela and Armand Lauffer with contributions by
Eugene Feingold and Ruben Meyer

Volume 10: **GROUP PARTICIPATION: Techniques for Leaders and Members**
by Harvey J. Bertcher

Volume 11: **BE ASSERTIVE: A Practical Guide for Human Service Workers**
by Susan Stone Sundel and Martin Sundel

Volume 12: **CHILDREN IN CRISIS: A Time for Caring, a Time for Change**
by Carmie Thrasher Cochrane and David Voit Myers

Volume 13: **COMMUNICATION IN THE HUMAN SERVICES: A Guide to
Therapeutic Journalism**
by Marcia S. Joslyn-Scherer

Volume 14: **NEEDS ASSESSMENT: A Model for Community Planning**
by Keith A. Neuber with William T. Atkins, James A. Jacobson,
and Nicholas A. Reuterman

Volume 15: **DEVELOPING CASEWORK SKILLS**
by James A. Pippin

Volume 16: **MUTUAL HELP GROUPS: Organization and Development**
by Phyllis R. Silverman

Volume 17: **EFFECTIVE MEETINGS: Improving Group Decision-Making**
by John E. Tropman

Volume 18: **AGENCY AND COMPANY: Partners in Human Resource Development**
by Louis A. Ferman, Roger Manela, and David Rogers

A **SAGE** HUMAN SERVICES GUIDE **15**

HV
43
·P53

DEVELOPING CASEWORK SKILLS

James A. PIPPIN

Published in cooperation with
the University of Michigan
School of Social Work

 SAGE PUBLICATIONS   Beverly Hills   London

GOSHEN COLLEGE LIBRARY
GOSHEN, INDIANA

To my granddaughter
Natasha Leah Pippin
June 10, 1977–January 7, 1979

Copyright © 1980 by James A. Pippin

All rights reserved. No part of this book may be reproduced or utilized in any form or by any means, electronic or mechanical, including photocopying, recording, or by any information storage and retrieval system, without permission in writing from the author and the publisher.

For information address:

SAGE Publications, Inc.
275 South Beverly Drive
Beverly Hills, California 90212

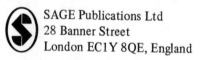

SAGE Publications Ltd
28 Banner Street
London EC1Y 8QE, England

Printed in the United States of America

Library of Congress Cataloging in Publication Data

Pippin, James A.
  Developing casework skills.

  (Sage human services guides ; v. 15)
  Bibliography: p.
  1. Social case work.   I. Title.   II. Series.
HV43.P53   361.3'2   80-18799
ISBN 0-8039-1503-9 (pbk.)

FOURTH PRINTING, 1985

CONTENTS

ABOUT THIS BOOK   9

INTRODUCTION   11

1. YOU AND YOUR CLIENT   15
   Becoming a Caseworker: Intentional? Accidental?   15
   A Public Welfare Client: What's It Like?   17
   Client Perceptions Are Shaped by the Community   18
   The Client Is Affected by Current Experience   19
   The Client Is Affected by the Availability of the Service   20
   The Office Environment Makes a Big Difference   21
   Summary   22
   Exercise   22

2. THE HELPING RELATIONSHIP:
   CORE HELPING CONDITIONS   23
   Relationship Makes the Difference   23
   Meeting Human Needs: Deepening and Fulfilling Social
      Caring and Responsibility   24
   The Helping Relationship Has Specific, Essential Components   26
   "Warmth-Respect"   26
   "Warmth-Respect" Affirms the Client's Intrinsic Value and Worth   27
   People's Views Are Extensions of Themselves   28
   Empathy Reaches Out, Tunes In, and Draws Out the
      Person's Emotions   29
   Empathy Can Be Learned and Developed   31
   Empathy Doesn't Mean a Loss of Objectivity   31
   Genuineness: A Clear Message About Yourself that
      Helps the Client   32

3. THE HELPING RELATIONSHIP:
   PROFESSIONAL GUIDELINES   35
   All Helping Relationships Are Not Professional Relationships   35

The Professional Relationship Is Always Purposeful 35
Professional Relationships Are Time Limited 36
Terminating the Casework Relationship Requires
    Delicate Handling 37
The Professional Relationships Is One Sided: It's for the Client,
    Not the Worker 39
Confidentiality Protects the Client's Right to Privacy 40
Caseworkers have No Privileged Information Protection 41
Confidentiality Means Informed Consent 41
Don't Take Sides 42
Don't Support Abuse 43
Working on Behalf of the Client in the Community 43
Summary 45
Exercises 45

4. THE SOCIAL WORK INTERVIEW
Core Conditions: Necessary but Not Sufficient 47
Interpersonal Communication with the Client:
    The Primary Objective 47
Communicating Accurately Requires
    One Sender and One Receiver 49
The Code: A Mixture of Words, Intotations, Inflections, Facial
    Expressions, and Gestures 50
The Code Transmitting the Message Is Not Always Consistent
The Interview: Dialogue and Monologue 53
Language Characteristics of a Piece of
    Communication Are Important 55
Qualitative Dimensions of Communication 56
Language: A Bridge or a Block? 57
Summary 58
The Interview: The Roles Are Clearly Defined 59
Phases of the Interview 61
Introductory Phase: Getting Acquainted and Agreeing About the
    Purpose of the Interview 61
Names Are Important 62
Clients Need Help in Feeling Important 63
Identify the Purpose of the Interview 64
The Less Verbal Client 65
Interpretation 66
The Skillful Use of Closed and Structured Open Questions
    Funnels the Clients Thinking Toward a Purpose 68

The Development Phase Explores the Problem in Depth 69
The Transition from the Developmental to the Ending Phase
  Should Be Clearly Recognized by Both Client and Worker 71
The Caseworker's Purpose Often Determines the
  Kind of Interview 72
Exercises 73

5. TASK-FOCUSED PROBLEM SOLVING 77
Problem-Solving Is Not Solution Giving 78
Solutions Must Be Personalized 78
The Task-Focused Problem-Solving Approach 79
Explaining the Process to the Client 80
Problem Exploration 81
Time Is Critical 83
Now Describe the Goal 84
The Contract: Oral or Written? 84
Problem Analysis Comes Next 85
Next, Formulate the Task 87
The Task Should be Feasible 88
The Task Should Be Desirable 88
Rehearsal 90
The Balance of the Process: Task Modification, Follow-Up,
  and Caseworker Assignments 91
Using the Task-Focused Approach with Long-Term Clients 92
Protective Service Cases: Special Consideration 93
Some Clients Refer Themselves or Are Referred and Can Identify
  No Target Problem 94
What If the Client Makes No Decision at the Conclusion of the
  Second Interview? 96
Evaluation: Have You Helped the Client? 97
Some Clients Are Not Helped 98
Exercises 98

6. PROBLEMS IN LIVING 101
Interpersonal Conflict 103
Difficulties in Role Performance 108
Reactive Emotional Distress 110
Inadequate Resources 112
Problems with Formal Organizations 115
Decision Problems 118
Summary 120
Exercise 121

7. CRISIS INTERVENTION   123
   Crisis: An Unexpected Problem in Living   123
   Premature Birth   125
   Role Changes and Loss of Status   127
   Rape   129
   Physical Illness   131
   Divorce   132
   Death of a Loved One   134
   Suicide   136
   Summary   137
   Exercise   138

8. WORKING WITH DIFFICULT CLIENTS   139
   Perhaps the Problem Is Differentness   139
   Differentness Comes from a Person's Environment   140
   Differentness May Be Shown by the Way a Person Meets Needs   141
   Differentness in Emotional Style, Personality, or Emotional
      Maturity May Generate Stress Between Client and Caseworker   143
   The Physical Characteristics of Client and Caseworker   145
   Exercise   148

9. TAKING CARE OF YOURSELF   151
   Exercise   153

NOTES   155

REFERENCES   155

QUESTIONNAIRE   157

ABOUT THE AUTHOR   159

ABOUT THIS BOOK

Jim Pippin has written the book that many of us wish we'd read during our first tough year in practice. While no introduction to casework can hope to cover every exigency, Pippin has managed to touch base with the major issues and to provide guidance to action in a remarkable variety of situations. Although he focuses on public welfare settings, readers in other fields will have no trouble transferring his suggestions to their practice.

Like other volumes in the series, *Developing Casework Skills* has been fully tested in dozens of settings. Experienced practitioners report that it is as useful to them for review purposes as it is to the untrained or experienced worker for purposes of introduction and orientation.

Armand Lauffer

Armand Lauffer, editor of the *Sage Human Service Guide* series is Professor of Social Work at the University of Michigan.

INTRODUCTION

This is a "how to" book on the practice of casework in a public social services agency. As such, it is intended to be a practical book—one providing specific information on skills and methods used in effectively working with clients. Although written for the novice in the field, seasoned workers may find some of the material helpful in better understanding or providing a new explanation for techniques already used successfully. In addition, supervisors may find here a useful resource in encouraging the professional growth of staff.

I do not believe that there is anything new in these pages. I have selected what I consider to be important concepts, techniques, and skills from the vast literature of social work and other helping disciplines. These I have translated into a blend of materials I consider essential to the competent practice of casework in a public services agency. To my knowledge, this has not been presented previously. I have tried to acknowledge those who proposed the seminal ideas from which the material is drawn. Any omissions are unwitting and deeply regretted.

Those who read this book will notice my intellectual debt to Helen Harris Perlman. Her most recent book, *Relationship: The Heart of Helping People*, was the model for Chapter 2. I was so impressed by her informal style that I attempted to address the reader similarly. The informed reader will notice also the influence of Alfred Kadushin in Chapter 4 on the social work interview. It should be obvious that Chapters 5 and 6 present an adaptation of the task-centered casework model of William Reid and Laura Epstein. My modifications are intended to provide a better fit with public welfare application. A major facet of my modification is an emphasis on relationship as well as task in every application of the casework model. My selection of the term "task-focused" is intended to reflect the presence of modifications.

A brief overview of the contents may be helpful. Chapter 1 considers the different worlds of the caseworker and the client as they come together in an interview. Chapter 2 outlines the necessary ingredients in a helping relationship and concludes with a set of guidelines which, when followed, convert a helping relationship into a helping professional relationship.

Chapter 3 provides an overview of how communication occurs between two people and how communication can be purposefully directed by a caseworker in an interview. Chapters 4, 5, and 6 are an overview and application of a task-focused approach to casework. The method is outlined in detail, followed by case examples of various problems faced by the typical caseworker. Included in these are problems related to crisis events as well as to long-standing conditions.

Chapter 7 takes a look at how unusual client behavior or needs create problems in the casework process. The concluding chapter addresses briefly the critical personal and professional issue—burnout. An appeal is made to the reader to take effective action on his or her own behalf in reducing the physical and emotional toll of helping needy people. Those interested in learning the art of empathy will be delighted with Pauline Lide's overview of her approach to learning this fundamental skill. It is included as the book's only appendix. At the conclusion of each chapter, a brief set of exercises is provided to stimulate the reader's thoughts regarding the use of the material presented.

Incidentally, I have chosen to use the female pronoun most of the time in writing these materials. This seems more appropriate to the majority of the reading audience for whom this book is intended. No slight to those of us who are male caseworkers is intended.

From the outset this has been a team project. Joyce Stringer and Mary Kingston of the Georgia Division of Family and

Children Services identified the need for such a book and attempted to recruit Pauline Lide, Associate Dean of the University of Georgia School of Social Work, to write yet another piece from her vast experience as a caseworker and teacher. I always will be grateful that Dr. Lide declined the offer in favor of my doing the writing with her as my consultant during the preparation. As I prepared materials, she read them and made suggestions for revisions. These revised pieces were submitted to Ms. Stringer and Ms. Kingston who made further comment. Their criticisms have greatly improved the quality of these materials. Those points of weakness which still remain, however, are solely my responsibility.

Others also contributed through their support and assistance. Sharolyn Griffin spent many hours typing the original manuscript and kept me encouraged with her enthusiastic comments regarding the readability of the material. Tom Morton, Director of the Office of Continuing Social Work Education at the University of Georgia and Betsy Lindsey of his staff, as well as Richard Lane who edited the prototype of this volume, *Casework in Public Social Services,* provided invaluable advice. Much of what has been added or changed from the prototype has come as a result of suggestions from Mr. Morton, Harriet Burns and Armand Lauffer, and to each I express a particular word of appreciation. To all of those who encouraged me in this effort I am deeply grateful, including especially Dean Charles A. Stewart of the University of Georgia School of Social Work who made the time available to me for this project. Funding for the prototype was provided by a grant to the Office of Continuing Social Work Education of the School of Social Work of the University of Georgia from the Georgia Division of Family and Children Services.

Finally, and most importantly, to my wife Elinor and my children, Archie, Steve, Richie, and Edie, I am deeply grateful. Without their encouragement and faith and willingness to endure the stress generated by such a project (which often meant delaying or putting aside their own needs), I would have fallen short of the necessary energy for completion.

1

YOU AND YOUR CLIENT

How do you feel about being a public welfare caseworker? A bit excited? Perhaps anxious? A tad disappointed? Maybe more ambivalent, uncertain, than anything else? Entering the world of public welfare strikes each of us in different ways, depending in part on our previous experiences and in part on our reasons for accepting the job.

Becoming a caseworker: intentional? accidental? During college I had a friend who was studying sociology and psychology. He was preparing for a career as a social case worker. I was studying physics and math, headed for nuclear engineering—I thought. I remember my friend's talking about how he had known since high school that he wanted to be a caseworker in a public welfare agency. He spoke warmly of a Sunday school teacher he had had at that time. She was apparently very enthusiastic about her work as a case worker and reflected a genuine sense of satisfaction in helping people. It took me a long time to realize that I wanted from my work the same satisfaction my friend knew he wanted and was preparing for. Perhaps that is the case with some of you. You never dreamed of being a public welfare caseworker . . . but here you are.

Many caseworkers tell me that they got into the job simply because there was nothing else available and because there were no specific qualifications or requirements for previous training in the field. If that's your position, you may well be a bit disappointed that nothing better was available—or relieved that you could get such a position without being specifically trained. No matter how you feel, your primary motive was your need for a job—which may mean you became a caseworker without asking yourself some important questions about the demands and rewards of the position.

Do I want to join with people in their misery and pain and help them to survive, and (it is hoped) to overcome their circumstances? Am I able to give of myself to another when the other may be not only unappreciative but also hostile? Can I feel pride in working in the public welfare system, or will I feel compelled to apologize and make excuses? Can I gain personal satisfaction from knowing I've done my job well, even when there seems to be no resultant, identifiable change in my client's life and circumstances? Do I really like people well enough to risk caring for them, even when it costs me more emotionally than I will ever receive in return?

There really aren't any magic answers to any of those questions. Rather, they alert those considering the profession to the personal costs to be anticipated as a public welfare caseworker. It is hoped that those of you who have known for some time that you have been headed in this direction have pondered these and similar questions and are aware of the demands implicit in people helping. Those for whom these questions raise surprisingly new concerns may wish to pause and reflect.

A special question: do you know what makes the profession attractive to you? Why do you want to help others? Is it that you feel sorry for the needy or poor? Perhaps you've been in circumstances where others depended on you and enjoyed the feeling you got then. Or is it a matter of values, your belief that everyone, rich or poor alike, deserves a chance in life? It's certainly not likely that your choice is motivated primarily by money. Though your salary will be adequate, it will not rival what you could earn in the business sector. If you are like others already in the profession, your attraction to social work has something important to do with your own, very personal, human needs.

Studies show that most persons in the helping professions are those with strong religious values; have a recognized need to be loved, accepted and needed; and tend to enjoy responsibility (many are senior siblings in their families of origin). The needs to be loved, accepted, and needed are very legitimate. They can be, and frequently are, strengths for the social caseworker, making possible higher levels of sensitivity, understanding, and empathy for the client, generating great satisfaction in the worker through the gains of the client.

But a caseworker must keep in mind that his or her needs, taken to extreme, likely will be destructive for the client. Frequently we need to inquire of ourselves regarding specific clients with whom we are working. Just how great is my need to be loved and accepted by this client? Have I so identified with the plight of this client that I have used her cause for a springboard to pursue what I think she needs and wants and determined to save her from her wretched condition without, in fact, listening to the uniqueness of her needs? Does it feel so good to have this client acknowledge my wisdom that I am constrained to give advice instead of encouraging independent thinking? Has this client come to need me—and I to need her needing me—so that I cannot let her discover she no longer needs me? Tough questions! But necessary ones that each caseworker must constantly ask herself if she is to stay alert to the traps our personal needs present in working with people.

A public welfare client: what's it like? What's it like to be a public welfare client? What's the client's point of view as she approaches and comes into contact with the department? Some of you may have been clients for brief crisis periods in your lives, perhaps even for extended periods in your early childhood. Compare your recollections and perceptions from that period with the description here. Consider sharing your perceptions with your colleagues. You'll very likely improve their understanding of their clients. You easily could tell them that there is no experience comparable to that of being a public welfare client. It's not like being a psychiatrist's patient or a lawyer's client; the public welfare client's experience is unique.

Client perceptions are shaped by the community. The experience of being a public welfare client actually begins in the community, not in the department's office. There is a message from the larger community, the society of which all Americans are a part. It says that economic self-sufficiency, self-reliance, and independence are sacred values to be held in honor and conformed to by all people, that recipients of welfare are probably lazy, good-for-nothing laggards. This message is confirmed by the surveys indicating that public welfare clients believe the larger community considers them bad or "sorry." Though the public norm is more accepting now of the poor elderly, many of them reflect feelings of shame and guilt that they no longer can care for themselves. Mothers of small children abandoned by their fathers are angry and hurt, often resentful, and almost always embarrassed as they request Aid to Families with Dependent Children. Even those who are seemingly caught in a cycle of dependence passed on from one generation to the next reflect the low self-esteem and poor self-concept of those condemned by the larger culture for their deviance. The condemnation does no good? Rather, it further alienates this small percentage of welfare recipients from people helpers who attempt to help them break the cycle. This message of society is rarely ever spoken directly to the clients; it simply envelopes them and defines them in relation to everyone else around him.

There are forces in the community that attempt to counter the message of the larger society. These forces tend to take shape in the neighborhood or immediate family of the client. Occasionally they take the form of organizations such as welfare rights associations and legal aid societies. In the case of the prospective client who has grown up in a family as a Public Welfare Dependent, the role of the client and the role of the caseworker are defined and imprinted in the mind of the person over many years. This person has been both directly and indirectly shaped by the behavior and attitudes of the adults with whom she has lived. She has learned either to trust or distrust the caseworker, to be condescending or aggressive, to be cooperative or hostile. The perceptions of this client are well formed and frequently imposed on the caseworker at the moment of first contact. No matter what these perceptions are, they potentially block effective communication between the client and the caseworker. If the worker is to change this perception, he or she must very accurately communicate his or her concern for and understanding of the client. Only a high level of empathy communicated over time in a relationship can reshape this client's warped perception.

In some cases, clients who come into the department have been coached by others in their family or in an organization about what they should say and do. Some clients are accompanied by organizational representatives or other family members. In these circumstances, it is difficult to develop a relationship with the client, and the overall experience easily leads to an antagonistic encounter.

Although few postsecondary students actually request services, a recent trend toward the use of food stamps during the financially pressing college years has brought an influx of middle-class persons into departmental offices. While this deviates from the societal norm of self-sufficiency, these persons are acting within their legal rights and receive much support from their peers, as well as from the contention that members of the middle class ought to get everything they can out of the system that they support or are likely to support with their taxes. (It is an enigma that this philosophy seems not to reduce the condemnation of society upon those briefly caught in a crisis and needing temporary but essential help.)

Obviously, the impact of the larger community and of the client's immediate family and neighborhood or peer group varies. However, it is always present and must be taken into account by the caseworker if she is to understand the client, particularly in the initial contact.

The client is affected by current experience. As the client enters the departmental office door she naturally brings already formed perceptions and expectations with her, but her feelings and thoughts about the problem or problems which bring her to the agency are paramount in her mind. There may be a single or primary focus. She has lost the part-time job she had. Her fourteen-year-old son has been caught shoplifting. Her baby is sick. Her utilities have been cut off. Hostilities with next-door neighbors have her afraid to go out of her house alone. Any one or a combination of unhappy circumstances could be happening in the life of a client, upsetting her and draining her of her energy. Each one might be labeled by the client as *the* problem, or the situation may be so confusing and overwhelming that the client has no "fix" on any one thing—just an awareness that everything is a mess, perhaps as usual. In the chapter on problems in living, careful attention will be given to understanding the dynamics of each of various problem configurations. At this point, we need simply to recognize that, in making contact with a client, the caseworker needs to be aware of the effect the client's current situation will make. She comes as a burdened person, or she would not come at all.

The client is affected by the availability of the service. For many welfare clients, an added problem is just getting to the departmental office. Although more counties are opening satellite offices to be more accessible to their clients, most provide only one location. Public transportation is not usually available, so clients beg or buy a ride, or walk. Mention is made of this added client hardship neither to accuse anyone nor to suggest that there are easy—or, in some circumstances, any—solutions. It is important, however, for the caseworker to realize that a welfare client frequently arrives at an interview feeling like I do when I get up to go to work, find my car battery dead, my next door neighbor already gone to work, no bus service in my area, and not enough cash in my pocket for a taxi. Under such circumstances, when I finally get to work I'm nearly worn out, my nerves are frayed, I'm a bit disgusted, and, all in all, I'm not really interested in dealing with anyone. Many of our clients enter the door to our county office feeling just like that.

The office environment makes a big difference. Once inside the door, the client, we hope, will find a less-demanding environment. I was recently in a county office in North Georgia where the waiting room was furnished with comfortable, attractive chairs and tables. A number of large green plants added life to the room. Recent issues of a variety of magazines, *People, Ebony, Parent's Magazine* and others, were on a table. The room spoke a message of welcome to clients. It offered some comfort for a moment's relaxation while waiting to see a caseworker. I complimented the county director on the attractiveness of the room. She responded, "I was determined this waiting room would not look like a welfare office." She added, "It took some getting used to. One child cried upon entering the door. She told her mother she didn't want to see the doctor."

A decor that permits people of many cultures to identify with at least something of the environment, a few magazines or some art work, together with a few things to keep children quietly involved, can make a great different in conditioning a client for a positive experience with a caseworker. Where these conditions do not exist, the waiting room simply adds to the stress. Clients sit and talk, frequently sharing their discontent. Frayed nerves are further stretched by crying children and cramped, uncomfortable, uninviting surroundings. The brief rest before the interview, a transition from the demands that preceded the client to the office, simply doesn't occur. More likely, irritations build and resentments grow. This, too, becomes a part of what the client brings into the interview with the caseworker.

Obviously, the potential that a client brings problems and stress into an interview is great. Perhaps it seems that the odds are against the caseworker engaging the client effectively. In some cases this is true, though with keen awareness and the patient use of understanding and skills, the caseworker may see even those very difficult cases move to more productive outcomes.

Summary. We've reviewed some of what the caseworker and the client bring to an interview setting when they sit together. Each brings his or her needs. Each brings a set of values and expectations that are primarily culturally determined. Each brings a predisposition toward relationship which stems from early experiences. The client, however, alone brings in her problem or problems to be looked at and, it is hoped, resolved. The caseworker is to leave her problems for consideration at another time with a colleague, friend, supervisor, or selected professional. If the interview is to be productive the caseworker must bring to the interview knowledge and skills that will enable a helping relationship to be effected with the client so that the client and her problem situation may be engaged. Our focus in the next chapter will be on that *helping relationship.*

Exercise

Think of two clients whom you serve or have served, one with whom you enjoyed working, and one with whom you had difficulty working. Write a brief statement describing the world of each client. In what respects are the lives of each similar and different? Look about your office and waiting room. What do you see that your client's might identify as signs of special welcome to each of them? What would you add or delete from the environment to better assure that a message of "welcome" is being conveyed?

_____

_____

_____

_____

2

THE HELPING RELATIONSHIP:
CORE HELPING CONDITIONS

Relationship makes the difference. I can feel the difference when the clerk responds to me rather than to my groceries. (I'm sure you've had the same experience.) Some do respond *only* to the objects in the basket, not speaking a word of greeting, nor even looking at me as I say, "Hi!" Mind you, I'm not looking for a conversation. Neither do I want a delay in processing my order, nor a distraction to increase the probability of an error. All I'm looking for is that little, but significant, difference that *relationship* makes.

And what a difference it makes! When the clerk catches my eye and smiles—saying something like, "Hello, do you have any coupons today?"—I feel good inside. At the least I feel noticed. More so, I feel related to this person, connected in a genuine, human, maybe even caring way. It takes only a few seconds for this contact to be established, for a message of warmth to be conveyed. Sometimes it seems as though some energy passes between the two of us. Whatever actually occurs, in those few seconds enough happens to make the business of getting my groceries checked and bagged an *uncommon experience.* Actually those few seconds influence my returning to that store. If I can, I'll choose that clerk's register the next time I'm in. That may mean she checks more customers, works a little harder; but I'll bet she also enjoys her work more than the worker who relates only to groceries, and not to people, all day long.

The difference in the two workers is relationship. One responded personally; the other depersonalized the interaction, adding nothing to me and perhaps even taking something from me. The worker who humanized the experience added to me. She gave me something of herself. Sure, it was only a bit; but every little bit of caring counts—at the grocery, the post office, or the county welfare office.

This difference between the two service providers in the grocery store is a part of what has been identified as the helping relationship. Whereas in the grocery store it is only an added plus and not essential to the service provided, for those of us who are professional care givers—social workers, nurses, doctors, or lawyers—the relationship *often does* make the difference in effectively providing the service. More about how later.

Meeting human needs: deepening and fulfilling social caring and responsibility. Helen Harris Perlman, in her book, *Relationship, The Heart of Helping People*, wrote, "This is what the human services in all their forms are for—to meet human needs in ways that deepen and fulfill the sense of social caring and responsibility between fellow human beings" (1979: 54). Although public welfare agencies, among the many agencies, groups, and individuals providing human services, appear to have less enthusiastic support in the broader community than most, we need to be reminded that the public welfare agency is *the* agency entrusted with our country's concern for the well-being of children and vulnerable adults. This is not simply a matter of practical necessity on the part of the community, as when the business leaders in a town set up a United Fund, one single gift to one fundraising agency, to avoid many groups' soliciting funds.

Rather, the public welfare agency is a direct expression of the values of our nation. There is a spirit of brotherhood that permeates the fundamental documents upon which this nation was founded. This same spirit brought into being many voluntary agencies such as family counseling centers, the Red Cross, and others. Each such agency plays a small but significant, additive role in the caring of the community for people in need.

But the central responsibility, the very trust of the nation, has been committed to the public welfare agency. It is the social caseworker in that agency, more than any other professional in the human services, who carries the responsibility to extend the hand of caring in the spirit of brotherhood to the outstretched hand of need.

As noted earlier, very, very few people like asking for help from any community agency, perhaps especially from the public welfare agency. Most people in that position are like a four cylinder automobile with only two cylinders working. That kind of trouble means that the car barely moves. Many applicants are operating at about one-half or less of their capacity. Ways of handling problems can easily break down or fall apart when one's survival needs, shelter, and food, are threatened. A helping relationship, a relationship that reaches out and supports, frequently enhances and restores the help seeker's coping capacities. The importance of the caseworker's response to the feelings of the client cannot be overemphasized. Apart from the client's feelings, most problems would appear to be routine— and in large measure similar to all other clients' problems. Feelings expressed by the client personalize the problem, make it uniquely hers. By responding in a helping fashion the caseworker touches the client's emotion of fear, embarrassment, exhaustion, whatever, and begins the regeneration of the client's energy and hope.

An appropriately used helping relationship also opens the way for the client to learn new ways of approaching difficult situations. Psychologists believe that learning takes place best in a warm, secure environment. We won't discuss in detail the very complex kinds of brain functions which go on inside our heads under these conditions. It is important, however, for the caseworker to realize that help seekers are sometimes so influenced by the caring caseworker that the client seems to take into herself a part of the worker. The caseworker in this instance can be a constructive resource in guiding the client to take the necessary risks that new learning demands. Obviously, this level of influence in the client's life, inappropriately used, has the potential for much harm: a sobering thought.

Learning occurs where the helping relationship is present and also through modeling. The client becomes impressed with the way the caseworker conducts herself. As the worker responds objectively to the client's problem, asks questions regarding various aspects of the problem situation, explores various alternatives available to the client, responds with respect to the client's ideas and solicits the client's opinions, the client begins to mirror the caseworker's ways of thinking, responding, and valuing. This learning is quite subtle, and often the client is not aware of it. However, it should not be unobserved by the caseworker. To take advantage of the modeling effect a caseworker sometimes needs to model specific behavior *intentionally*. As the caseworker observes occasional role reflections, she may choose to reinforce this new learning—this newly acquired behavior or attitude—through an appropriate role play or a favorable comment with the client. Appropriate use of influence or modeling with the client is a part of what social workers refer to as "the appropriate use of self in a helping relationship." Such appropriate ways of responding do indeed "meet human needs in ways that deepen and fulfill the sense of social caring and responsibility between fellow human beings." It is through this process, more than any other, that the caseworker fulfills her public trust to embody the spirit of brotherhood.

The helping relationship has specific, essential components. There is agreement among the helping disciplines that a set of core conditions essential to the helping relationship exists. One facet we call "warmth-respect" includes what others have labeled as acceptance, caring-concern, positive regard, and non-judgmental attitude. Another is empathy; and a final one is genuineness, sometimes identified as congruence. These refer both to the attitude and behavior of caseworkers. As each is examined, illustrations are provided which flesh out the idea and indicate how clients get a sense of the caseworker's warmth-respect, empathy, and genuineness in the professional relationship.

Warmth-respect. There is a spontaneity about some people that seems to reach out and touch others in the kind of contact which, even for the briefest of moments, feels warm and good.

It feels natural and right. It seems like what being human has to be about. Those who have tried to define warmth have spoken of a subjective inner condition not readily identified by someone who is merely observing an interaction. Studies of video tapes of workers judged to be warm by their clients suggest that warmth is communicated primarily through nonverbal expressions. As the worker speaks, the tone of voice (rather than the actual words), the facial expression, the gestures used, the body posture (leaning slightly forward), and sometimes the act of physically touching: All or part, in varied combinations, are experienced by the client as warmth. In fact, one study suggests that smiling is the best single predictor of the client's identifying the worker as warm.

"Warmth-respect" affirms the client's intrinsic value and worth. Acceptance, nonjudgmental attitude, caring-concern, positive regard, and respect are concepts deeply rooted in the notion that human beings have dignity and worth. This permeates our society, touches the very origin of this nation, and is repeatedly reflected in the Constitution and the Bill of Rights. Social workers have long pointed to the importance of accepting the client "as he really is, including his strengths and weaknesses, his congenial and uncongenial qualities, his positive and negative feelings, his constructive and destructive attitudes and behavior, maintaining all the while a sense of the client's innate dignity and personal worth, (Perlman, 1979: 99). As such, acceptance has never been intended as approval, of either constructive or destructive client actions or attitudes. What is essential is that the client experiences herself as being respected by the caseworker.

An examination of Carl Rogers's "unconditional positive regard" is helpful. Although Rogers's own definition seems a bit mystical and hard to grasp, studies of video-taped interviews with Rogers demonstrating "unconditional positive regard" show that he maintains a constant emphasis on the positive assets of the client. "From a first glance, one would think that the client has no assets, no hope. But, out of a dark morass of discouragement, Carl Rogers seems always to find something positive in an individual" (Ivey and Autnier, 1978: 132) and highlights that positive dimension by responding to it. "By focusing on the positive dimensions . . . Rogers is merely directing attention to what people already know and are" (Ivey and Autnier, 1979: 133). This positive focus is illustrated in the following interaction:

> **Client** (angrily): The next time he lies to me I'm going to slap him into next week!
>
> **Worker**: You're very upset and concerned about him and feel you must do something to stop this behavior.

Although slapping her son "into next week" is not behavior which the worker can approve or support, she can pick up on the mother's expressed intention and desire to take *some* responsibility for dealing with the problem she and her son have. By selectively responding to this positive, forward-moving aspect of the interaction the worker has preserved the dignity and worth of the client which would have been challenged had she responded in a blaming or accussing fashion to the anger and what may well be viewed by the worker as intended brutality or abuse. The worker's response can then move toward exploring ways of stopping the behavior. The response of the worker generates in the client a sense of being respected, because it credits the client's intention and demonstrates an underlying assumption—that this client aims to be helpful to herself and to others and that she has the potential to do so. Recognizing the positive assets of our clients and communicating these to them is at the very heart of the warmth-respect concept.

People's views are extensions of themselves. Another aspect which needs to be noted before we leave warmth-respect is how the worker can respond to ideas and views which differ from her own. All of us have experienced making a suggestion or expressing an opinion and being put down by someone who viewed things differently. "Being put down" is the opposite of being respected. Showing respect for another person is directly connected with how one handles that person's ideas. It is as if the person's ideas are really a piece of the person. Treating the ideas as unimportant, stupid, or irrelevant designates the person as unimportant, stupid, or irrelevant. The same is true of being flippant or teasing with a person's words when the person intended them as serious. One's views and opinions are an extension of oneself. Ideas given in a serious vein have an implicit tag attached: "Please handle with loving care." Following this prescription would improve greatly the worker's probabilities of developing a helping relationship, especially with clients of a different culture. Ivey and Authier suggest two basic types of comments that communicate respect where differences of opinion, or different world views, exist. One he calls *enhancing* and the other *appreciation of differences.*

Enhancing statements include "You express your opinion well" and "Good insight." Appreciation of difference statements include "I don't see it that way, but I can imagine how you could arrive at that opinion" and "I may disagree with what you say, but I will support your right to say it," [1978: 136].

More attention will be given to the various aspects of being different and its implications for the helping relationship in the subsequent section on culture.

Empathy reaches out, tunes in, and draws out the person's emotions. Closely related to warmth-respect is the notion of *empathy.* "This means feeling *with* and *into* another person, being able to get into his shoes. It may occur spontaneously or may be carefully learned 'listening with the third ear' and responding in tune with the other person" (Perlman, 1979: 57). Carl Rogers wrote, "To sense the client's private world as if it were your own, but without losing the 'as if' quality—this is empathy" (1961: 284).

Each of us has at some time had someone say to us, "I know just how you feel." Such an expression is a reflection of sympathy, not empathy. The statement does reflect emotion and may well touch the emotion of the client, reflecting a bond of caring-concern; but it is sympathy, and not empathy, because it reflects the speaker's feelings—which she assumes are the same as yours. Empathy makes no such assumption but reaches out, tunes in, and draws out the person's emotion to identify it for the person. It is this reflection of another's emotion, and communication of it back to its owner, that we define as empathy.

The intent of the sympathetic person is to let the other know "how sorry I feel for you." The empathic person wants the other to know "I am with you. I understand how *you* feel." Notice that the empathic person wants the other to get the *message* "I know how you feel." Those words need not be spoken at all, but the message—"I know how you feel"—comes through as one's feelings are tuned in on, touched, reflected back, and identified in the tone of voice, facial expression, and words of the empathic person.

The following exchanges illustrate both sympathetic and empathic responses to the same client expression:

> **Client**: I just don't know what I'm going to do, losing my part-time job, what with Christmas coming up.
>
> **Worker**: I'd be angry, too. I can't imagine anyone's laying off anybody the week before Christmas!

The worker responded to her own feelings, what she assumed the client was feeling. But she was wrong about her client's feelings. Look what an empathic response reveals about the client.

> **Client**: I just don't know what I'm going to do, losing my part-time job, what with Christmas coming up.
>
> **Worker**: You're pretty upset! You even seem afraid of something, or someone. Is that it?
>
> **Client**: Yeah, sort of. I'm afraid I won't have the money to get the kids' Christmas out of lay-away.

The empathic response of this worker has exposed the most immediate problem of the client. It's not the loss of the job but the problem the job loss precipitates that the client is facing. Responding to the supposed anger fails to deal with the client where she is.

Empathy can be learned and developed. Empathy seems to come naturally for some people. But for the most of us who don't have the skill, training is available. Pauline Lide has developed a procedure that caseworkers can use for developing what she calls "a dynamic mental representation" of the client (Lide, 1967: 23-30). A detailed explanation is in the Appendix and will aid the interested reader in improving the empathic quality of his responses. Other approaches to learning empathy, approaches that focus more on the kinds of verbal responses the caseworker makes to the client, have also been developed. Ivey points out that verbalizations which reflect the client's emotions and thoughts, coupled with nonverbal components such as eye contact, slightly leaning forward, appropriate facial expression, and the like, have been identified in video-tape recordings as important in displaying high levels of empathy. These particular verbal and nonverbal responses are covered in detail in the Appendix as well.

Empathy doesn't mean a loss of objectivity. Objectivity has consistently been raised as a concern where empathy is taught to caseworkers. If the worker gets into the client's shoes, how does she know where she herself stands? Some cite the common problem of overreacting to the client's problem or of getting so emotionally involved with the client that the caseworker takes over the problem from the client. True, even the most seasoned professional can find she is getting more and more caught up in a client relationship. This sort of overinvolvement has been called "wallowing in the relationship." I like that phrase because it graphically describes the red flags that should alert the professional to an inappropriate client relationship. "Wallowing" suggests staying in one place, going nowhere. This is different from feeling stuck, since wallowing is generally considered to be a pleasurable experience for a pig (and, I'm suggesting, an equally pleasurable experience for caseworkers who've lost their objectivity).

Objectivity enables the caseworker to respond to her client warmly and empathically while, without losing touch, stepping back and asking: "Where are my client and I headed right now? What do my own feelings tell me about our relationship? Do I so look forward to seeing my client that it's the highlight of my day, or do I so dread to see this client that I keep hoping she won't show up?" Objectivity is simply the discipline of the professional to account to herself about how helpful the relationship is to the client and how helpful specific responses are or will be for the client. Where the conclusion of the caseworker regarding impact on client is uncertain—or is a definite "destructive!"—then the worker must refrain from the response and more carefully monitor the direction in which she is moving the client.

Genuineness: a clear message about yourself that helps the client. Genuineness, the final component of the core conditions for a helping relationship, has to do with how things fit together and form a whole. Think of a person as a picture cut into parts like a jigsaw puzzle. Although the person is a whole, what we get as we have contact with the person are glimpses—pieces of the picture. As we relate to the person we begin to put the picture together. We should begin to get a sense of the whole with only a few pieces. There should be a fit between various parts and among them all. This fit is sometimes called congruence. Genuineness in relationship has to do with the fit of what a person expresses of himself or herself in various ways at various times. If the various expressions, both verbal and nonverbal, give one a sense of a whole, then we say the person is genuine, or congruent, with himself or herself.

Genuineness, then, is an absence of contradictory messages from the person about herself. Genuineness is the opposite of falseness, phoniness, or fakery. Phoniness is usually recognized when a person says one thing verbally but simultaneously reflects an entirely different message on the nonverbal level, through voice tone, facial expression, or other body responses. Also, friends of long standing may recognize phoniness in one another when what a person professes is in direct contradiction to the consistent values, attitudes, and actions that person has expressed over time. Genuineness, then, has to do with being free of pretension, being whole, being put together.

To be totally genuine with oneself is probably impossible. The required self-awareness—being tuned in on oneself at all times—is more than most of us have yet learned to do. But our deficiencies in this regard do not diminish the importance of the goal. Strive to be genuine! There are two facets to genuineness in a helping relationship. The first has to do with the genuineness with oneself which we have just been discussing, the second with genuineness in response to one's client—*how* the worker's responses fit with the client's expressions of ideas and feelings.

Genuineness with oneself as a professional means not taking on the "air of professionalism," not hiding behind the facade of degrees and credentials. This kind of genuineness demands that the responses the worker makes to her client accurately represent the worker. Note the differences in the illustrations below:

> **Client:** I was wondering if you could let me have five dollars until next week. We're completely out of food.
>
> **Worker** (fidgeting anxiously): I wish I could, but we aren't supposed to loan clients money. I'd be glad to otherwise.

or

> **Worker** (fidgeting anxiously): You caught me a bit by surprise. I really don't know how to answer you. I'm really concerned that you're out of food, but I don't think it would be good if I loaned you money out of my own pocket. But I do want to see that you have some food before the day is over.

The first worker was full of contradictions. The client could get no sense of who the worker was, only that something was wrong. The client is left in a dilemma: "Does the worker care whether or not my children and I starve, or did I do something wrong to offend her?"

The second worker responds openly, but not destructively, to the client. She expresses her surprise, her thoughts about the appropriateness of acting affirmatively on the client's request, expresses concern for the client, and commits to helping the client resolve the dilemma. It's important that notice be given to the *constructive* yet open response of the worker. Being totally honest might have meant telling the client that she, the worker, was behind on her rent, had only a dollar in her pocket, and didn't know how she would make it to the end of the month. Such a disclosure would have been destructive to the client-worker relationship and would have inappropriately burdened the client with the worker's problems.

Elizabeth Ivey has suggested that "the person who is synchronous or genuine within the self is most likely focused. . . . Genuineness in relationship requires attention to the self *and* to the other" (Ivey and Authier, 1987: 151). This is the second aspect of genuineness referred to earlier: how the worker's responses fit with the client's expressions of ideas and feelings. The word *synchronous* describes the desired responses of the worker. In observing the client-worker interaction, an overall fit in the communication should be occurring. Both the client and the worker would be mirroring one another's postures, movements, and voice tones. This unconscious mirroring of behavior suggests a level of communication between the two that goes beyond their immediate awareness. The two are so tuned in to each other that they move in unison, as two ice skating partners. Studies of audio tapes indicate a similar congruence of vocal tone and tempo where genuineness between two persons is present.

Among the three—warmth-respect, empathy, and genuineness—genuineness may well be the most important. Warmth-respect and empathy will not go far if the client gets a sense of the worker's withholding herself, presenting mixed messages about herself, or dividing her attention between the client and other people or things during the course of an interview. On the other hand, the worker who is finely tuned in to her client will heighten the sense of warmth experienced and increase the probability of the client's hearing the worker's empathic response of understanding.

3

THE HELPING RELATIONSHIP:
PROFESSIONAL GUIDELINES

All helping relationships are not professional relationships.
Our discussion has been illustrated with references to worker-
client relationships, since that is the focus of this book. But I'm
sure you've experienced empathy, warmth, and genuineness
from certain friends, relatives, or colleagues. Helping relationships are not limited to professional contacts. In fact, studies
have shown that professionals don't always form helping relationships. That's a professional and personal deficit no reader
has to be satisfied with. Awareness is the first step toward
improvement. Careful application of the empathy training procedures in the Appendix is the second step. Conscientious
practice will bring about the desired results for the caseworker.
For the helping relationship to be professional as well, certain
guidelines must be followed.

*The professional relationship is always purposeful: the goals
have been identified and agreed to by the client.* Social casework
places a high priority on guaranteeing the client the right of
self-determination. Practically speaking, this means that the
caseworker and the client work together in a very straightforward and aboveboard fashion. The purpose of the relation-

ship is to resolve some problem that the client has in obtaining necessary services or material means or a problem in personal coping or interpersonal relationships. The caseworker, with the client, identifies what it is the two are to try to resolve together. Contrary to the practice of some caseworkers, there should be no hidden agenda, no goals toward which the worker is striving which have not been both recognized and agreed upon by the client. In the discussion, the client will explore many facets of her life as she describes the problem. By now each of us has come to realize that there are no simple problems—especially if you are the one having the problem. Particularly where survival issues such as food and shelter or health are involved, emotions transform the situation into a complex drama, often with a sense of life or death consequences. True, the client's reaction may be out of proportion to the seriousness of the situation as seen through the eyes of the caseworker; but the problem for the caseworker is always the person in the midst of his or her situation. Carefully the dilemma must be explored, so that the agreed upon goals address both the client's reaction *and* the situation to which the client is reacting.

Professional relationships are time limited. The relationship between the client and the caseworker is by definition time limited from the very start. It begins with a client's need or needs which the caseworker and client formulate into a goal or set of goals. The relationship ends as the goals are accomplished or as it becomes clear that the casework relationship has contributed all that can be realistically expected.

Sometimes it is difficult to translate a goal or set of goals into an expected period of time. This is true particularly with problems involving difficulties with interpersonal relationships. Some of your clients will have family problems, perhaps child-rearing or marital difficulties. Conflicts with neighbors or school officials are not unusual. Whereas assistance in securing better housing or following up on a medical service problem may be predicted as requiring one or more weeks, interpersonal problem situations are quite unpredictable. In such cases it is important that short-term objectives—steps along the way toward the goal—be established. Occasional reference to these steps keeps the relationship focused and provides opportunities to evaluate programs.

Occasionally it becomes apparent that no progress is being made. The caseworker should be well aware of this fact through supervisory and self-review. Some professional judgment should have been exercised prior to the next casework interview to plan how best to explore this with the client. Many factors can be involved where progress is not being made. The caseworker and the client may simply have not been able to form a cooperative relationship. The client may have had other demands arise, demands which now take precedence over the previously agreed upon problem. Or there may be a lack of caseworker knowledge and expertise in the problem area. These situations call for a change, perhaps to a more appropriate goal, to another caseworker or a more knowledgeable professional, or to a specialist in the problem area. Some of these changes mean a termination of the casework relationship. Such a change is a delicate matter and requires careful handling.

Terminating the casework relationship requires delicate handling. No matter what the circumstances for terminating the client-worker relationship, it is a delicate matter due to the emotions involved both on the part of the client and on the part of the caseworker. The often quoted line, "No man is an island," relates to the connectedness of the people. Any person's loss is a loss to another. Perhaps the greatest loss is the connectedness. This is true even when the relationship has not accomplished its intended goals. Early in my professional career, I learned, first-hand, the truth in these words.

Sue S. was nineteen, very shy and very lonely. She came to the family service agency where I worked for help in dealing with her creditors. She was recently divorced and supported her two-year-old-son by working as a machine operator in a textile plant. It seemed so easy to respond to her hurt and assure her of my support in her efforts to survive as a single parent. Eagerly she entered the interview each time she arrived, telling me about her week and always noting how important seeing me was to her. "You are my only real friend," she often said. Always I assured her what a pleasure it was to see her, and it was.

As I continued to carry the case I became more and more uneasy over what seemed to me an inappropriate kind of dependence that seemed to be growing. I was alarmed that I was handling my relationship with this client poorly and that little had changed in her life since we began work together—she still had creditor problems, and she had no friends except me. I could see I was little or no help to her. After a brief discussion with other staff members, I decided that I should transfer Sue S. to another caseworker. In our next interview together I explained to her that I had been all the help I could be and felt that she needed someone new as a caseworker. She sat quietly looking at her hands in her lap. Her face showed surprise and hurt. She murmured very quietly, "I will miss you—you've been very nice." I realized she was about to cry and suggested she could meet her new worker, adding "I will miss you, too." She said she had only a few minutes as she was coming by to tell me she could not keep her appointment due to another appointment. I introduced her to her new worker as she left and they made an appointment for the following week—but she did not keep it. Efforts to get her to return were fruitless.

A casework relationship should never be ended abruptly. Both the client and the worker need time to prepare for the termination; it involves both appreciating one another for the "connectedness" you've had and grieving about the loss of contact in the future. ("Grief" may be a rather strong word here, but more than likely there will be expression of regret and sadness that the time to be spent together will soon be concluded.) This typically involves some reminiscing about both the difficult and the productive parts of working together. This enables both the client and the worker to get a new perspective on their work, a perspective that is an essential part of the evaluation for the worker. On an emotional scale, this sharing allows the two to move from the intimacy of need and dependence to the respect for emotional distance entailed in interdependence. Handled in this fashion, closure leaves a warm glow of caring accompanied by a taste of satisfaction.

The case of Sue S. illustrates the unresolved feelings, the lack of understanding, and the hurt which accompany relationships which are severed rather than diminished and then terminated. The preparatory process for termination needs to be engaged in even when the relationship has not accomplished its goal or goals. The client and the caseworker have been investing energy in each other; concluding this relationship, no matter how productive, involves a redirection of that energy. This can best be accomplished where the energy can be slowly or at least thoughtfully withdrawn rather than being left open like a faucet spilling water aimlessly on the ground.

The process of termination is built into time-limited casework, since a goal is designated and an approximate amount of time is agreed on to work toward that goal. The client knows from the beginning that there will be an end. James Mann (1973), a proponent of time-limited client contact, suggests that the time limitation be in terms of the number of interview contacts rather than a specific date. The worker and client are to keep aware of how many contacts have been made and how many remain to accomplish the goals. This focus on the passing of time motivates both the client and the worker to use well this time together. He points out that, by the middle of the mutually designated interviews, the client reminds the worker that termination is forthcoming. Thus, preparation for concluding the relationship, together with a very important mechanism for increasing motivation, is built into the casework.

The professional relationship is one-sided; it's for the client not the worker. That probably seems obvious enough on' the surface. It is the client who presents the problem to be worked on. But it does not always feel like it should be that way, particularly with a client who demands a great deal and gives nothing in return. Many clients enter a casework relationship because they have run out not only of material but also human resources. The people around them who would ordinarily support and sustain them no longer meet that need. Perhaps the client has geographically got out of touch with them; or, worse, perhaps those sustaining persons have withdrawn their support and rejected the client. Persons hungry for relationship drink long at the well of the caseworker before even acknowledging to the worker that they have been drinking.

Somehow or another, someone in the past supported the notion that there were "good" clients and "bad" clients. "Good" clients show appreciation and are grateful for the services rendered; "bad" clients take the service for granted and demand "more than they deserve." The caseworker's experience of being drained easily supports the notion that something's wrong with the relationship, that in some way the client isn't fulfilling her part of the bargain. There is no exchange trade-off in the professional relationship. There are no guarantees to the worker beyond the fulfillment of personal professional aspirations and the compensation of employment benefits, money, vacation, in-service training, and other fringe benefits. When the casework relationship is productive for the client, when the client invests herself in remedying her problem or is able to give feedback on progress or demonstrate a step forward, then the worker does experience a return of energy, a surge of satisfaction from the client. *Note,* however, that this is not in the bargain. It is only a secondary gain, not required of the client, though hoped for and expected *on the client's behalf.*

Confidentiality protects the client's right to privacy. Since the professional relationship is for the client, there are some rules which guarantee the client's rights. The most important of those is confidentiality. This is a very complex rule which takes on an even more complex nature as it is applied in the public welfare agency. In its simplest form, confidentiality means that all that takes place between the professional and the client is the property of the client and cannot be publicized in any way. We may assume that such secret keeping on the part of the professional is simply a matter of ethics, good faith on the part of the professional. At its heart, it probably is. Unfortunately, it is not a matter of law, as most of us have assumed. Ministers, social workers, counselors, and even doctors have only limited protection of the law allowing them to withhold information about their clients. In the state of Georgia only lawyers and psychologists have laws protecting their client relationship as being privileged. In a court of law only these two professions have the right not to disclose information regarding their clients. Recent legislation requiring reports of child abuse abridge even those rights.

*Caseworkers have no privileged information protection.*In the public welfare agency, confidentiality does not mean that all that takes place in the casework relationship is the property of the client. We need to remember that the caseworker has no relationship with the client other than that sanctioned by the agency. The help seeker is the agency's client. The caseworker is the agent of the agency. Anything that the caseworker is privy to, the agency is privy to as well. What transpires with the client needs to be understood by the client as being available to the caseworker's supervisor and, if recorded in the client's record, available to other administrative persons in the agency, and eventually to any agency personnel who might at a later date read the record. This obviously has implications for what is written into a client's record. If the caseworker should be called to testify in court, nothing that has taken place in the relationship, nor anything that is written in the record, is considered by the court to be privileged. A caseworker who refuses to answer the questions of the court could easily find herself in the same position as the New York *Times* reporter who refused to disclose to the court a source of information. He spent a lot of time in jail on a contempt of court charge.

Confidentiality means informed consent. The rule of confidentiality in the public welfare agency means that the client can expect the caseworker to exclude any reference to her in informal conversations with other agency personnel, over coffee, in passing, or in other situations not directly connected with meeting the client's goals. The client can expect that no reference regarding her will be made to other clients without her expressed permission. This rule holds even when the other client is a member of the client's immediate or extended family. The client can expect that no communications regarding her or on her behalf will be made with personnel of other agencies without her expressed permission. Certainly any written communication outside of the agency referring to the client ought to be covered by a specific (not a blanket) release of information regarding the specific communication. This is a much more rigid application of the rule of confidentiality in casework than Perlman suggests: "That he will transmit no information to anyone except as it is to be *for* the client, in his best interests, to further his problem-solving efforts (Perlman, 1979: 70).

Perlman's position seems to be based on the practical necessity of the worker's dealing with personnel in other agencies from which the client is receiving services or needs to secure services. Such exchanges are typically verbal but should still be covered by a release of information specifying the agency to be communicated with and the range of information required. Every effort should be made to assure that all disclosures are made with the client's informed consent. Careful attention to this client right keeps both the client and the caseworker aware that, though there is a high level of trust and liking between the two, theirs is a professional relationship. In order not to hamper the caseworker's contact with other helping professionals, the necessary releases can be obtained during the early part of the relationship when the problem is being defined and information is being gathered. Collaborative agencies can be identified, explored with the client regarding the need for contact, and included in the service plan for caseworker action. Perlman's "best interest" definition is unnecessarily broad.

Don't take sides. Mention has been made of occasions in which more than one member of a family might be the clients of the same caseworker. This can pose some real problems for the caseworker, especially where the goals of one or more of the clients relate to resolving interpersonal difficulties within the family. Caseworkers are expected to be advocates for their clients, and the assumption is that the interests of any two or more clients will not conflict with each other.

Such a conflict exists, however, when an adolescent daughter wants her rules at home relaxed and her mother wants her to obey the rules as they are. Here the caseworker does well to make it clear to all clients that her function is not to take sides, to be an advocate for either party with the other; rather, she will support each as a solution is sought either through arriving at a new understanding or identifying a specialist who can assist with greater knowledge and experience. It is important that the caseworker in intervening in a family recognize that the individual cultural differences of families must be respected. This can best be done by limiting casework tactics to encouragement and clarification of communication between family members. If this doesn't help, the family should be assisted in securing the services of a specialist in family counseling. If the referral is to be acted on by the family, all must sense a positive relationship with the caseworker.

Don't support abuse. The one exception to the "don't take sides" rule is where the physical or emotional safety of a family member is in jeopardy. In cases of physical abuse, the worker should leave no doubt that inflicting injury on another is absolutely inexcusable and must be stopped permanently. In taking this position the caseworker has the full support of society's law. Emotional abuse, however, is not so easily judged. Adults must learn to resolve this dilemma themselves through more effective coping and interpersonal skills. Where a child appears to be emotionally abused, the caseworker should call attention to her concern and insist on a referral to a competent specialist if the suspected abuse continues. As the worker does this, she risks losing a positive relationship with one or more members of the family, but to do otherwise jeopardizes the safety of one individual and violates the public trust the worker holds.

Working on behalf of the client in the community. An essential—perhaps *the* essential—element of casework is the work one does on a client's behalf with other people in the community. These contacts range from those with other professionals such as physicians, attorneys, and school teachers to those with volunteers in the community organizations or occasionally members of the person's neighborhood. This part of the casework is extremely important, since many of the client's emotional and service needs can best be met in the larger community or the client's neighborhood. To be successful in this regard the caseworker must intentionally cultivate relationships with colleagues in other service agencies and with contacts in volunteer organizations who may be of assistance to clients.

The same core conditions required for a helping relationship pay off in developing collegial relationships. There is no substitute for warmth-respect, empathy, and genuineness in becoming a helpful colleague of other professionals. Most of us hurt from time to time from bumps with clients, in our organizations, or with other professionals. Finding another professional who listens empathically and confidentially inevitably leads to an improved working relationship on behalf of our clients. And when we support other professionals we generally find them supportive of us as well. Such a supportive network is considered to be the best hedge against caseworker "burn out," a significant problem in today's work force.

Occasionally you have to deal with personnel in your own agency, or in other agencies, on behalf of a client. The best way to approach this person is to assume that he or she is as interested in your client's well-being as you are. Never suggest that you are meeting your responsibility as an advocate for your client. The notion of advocacy is claimed by most professionals, not just social workers. Use diplomacy, be empathic, warm, and genuine, not syrupy-sweet; but in good caseworker style, start where this person is, as if he or she were a client. After establishing rapport, move on to being more specific about your client's needs, inquiring if the specific services rendered by the person can be made available to the client. Remember, in this instance, pushing client rights may win the battle, but lose the war for a client. A hostile intake worker in another agency can create all kinds of delays in making a service available. Your client doesn't need delays. In the slang of another year, when it comes to referrals the caseworker is expected "to grease the wheels of bureaucracy." Of course, if this doesn't work, then other means will have to be pursued.

Summary. The core conditions of warmth-respect, empathy, and genuineness are essential to the helping process. But they are not alone sufficient. A professional relationship should also be: (1) directed toward the client's goals; (2) time-limited; (3) focused on meeting the client's, not the worker's, needs; (4) confidential; (5) balanced where more than one family member is involved; and (6) useful in securing community services for the client.

Exercises

Often the caseworker is a model for her client. Which of your behaviors or attitudes do you think serve as important models for your clients? List them below.

_____

_____

_____

_____

Think about one of your clients. Create a picture in your mind —how she feels, what she thinks, what she wants. Describe your mental picture.

_____

_____

_____

_____

GOSHEN COLLEGE LIBRARY
GOSHEN, INDIANA

The caseworker must respect and protect the client's right of privacy. In what way is confidentiality observed in your agency? Do these procedures adequately protect your client? What changes would you make in the procedures?

_____

_____

_____

_____

Caseworkers have frequent contact with other professionals. Think of a recent contact and examine the effect of that contact on you, the other professional, and your mutual client. What happened in the contact that made it beneficial to you, to the other professional, or to your client. Note also anything that seemed to detract from a positive contact.

_____

_____

_____

_____

4

THE SOCIAL WORK INTERVIEW

The core conditions: necessary but not sufficient. Empathy, warmth-respect, and genuineness, as previously discussed, are necessary conditions for a helping relationship; but these conditions are not sufficient for a professional relationship to be productive. When I last selected a dentist I asked neighbors, colleagues, and various other friends whom each would recommend. Inevitably in the course of the reply reference would be made to how "painless" the dentist was. Of course, mention was also made regarding the dentist's fees and the case of obtaining an appointment. I equated in my mind the idea of "painlessness" with the notion of competence. I selected my dentist, and as I was sitting in his chair on my first visit I commented to him that he had come highly recommended as being "painless." He laughed and noted he did have what he called "good technique." He explained that good technique meant knowing the most effective painkilling drug to use, knowing precisely where the nerve centers for the teeth are located, being able to look at the gum structure of the tooth root, and having the skill to inject the drug precisely in that specific place. I was impressed. "Painless" certainly sounded like competence to me. But I learned more about competence in his chair that day.

As he took a good look at my teeth he commented on the fillings which had previously been done. He noted that I had apparently had some since childhood. He was right. He further noted that they were "a work of art," and said, "Your dentist really had good technique." There was that word again: "technique." Perhaps it is good technique, not just "painlessness," that relates to competence. After all, what difference does it make if it didn't hurt if the fillings fall out in a few weeks or months?

For the social worker, competence involves many forms of knowledge, capacity to understand and make judgments, and a variety of skills. Of the many competencies we will consider, none is more important nor more essential than knowing what takes place in an effective interview and being able to put into practice that knowledge in a meeting with a client. The social work interview is the primary means of communicating with a client about her needs and of bringing into being a plan of action on her behalf. How the client experiences the interview as a productive process guided by the worker will in large measure determine how competent the client perceives the worker. Interview technique is to the social worker what "painless" technique is to the dentist, an impression-making and useful *part* of the intervention—*but not all of it.*

Interpersonal communication with the client: the primary objective. Communication is one person's sending a message and another person's receiving the message sent. Sounds simple—but it isn't! Let's take the simple message, "I'm hungry!" The person wishing to send the message is a six-month-old baby, Sara. Sara wishes to convey to her mother the message, "I'm hungry!" She must put this message into a code. The typical code for people usually consists of a combination of words and gestures. However, since Sara has not yet learned any words, her code consists of a scream accompanied by specific facial gestures and arm movements that her mother decodes as "I'm hungry!" Through words, gestures, voice intonation, and perhaps touching, Sara's mother encodes a message back to her— "You're hungry!"—which Sara decodes, followed by encoding another message through a slight change of pitch, variations of intensity, and different gestures, which might carry the message, "I'm glad you heard." Or maybe, "Hurry up!" Such is the magic of mothering, but what if Sara's mother had been away and a babysitter had come in? Sara would encode the same message sound and gestures, but the babysitter might decode the message as "I'm wet!" or "I'm hot!" or "I'm tired!" or any number of other similar messages. Why? She doesn't know Sara's code. Miscommunication of this sort is typical with a new babysitter. It is also quite common where any two persons attempt to send messages to each other, particularly where the two persons are new acquaintances or have infrequent contact.

Communicating accurately requires one sender, and one receiver. When two people communicate there is a natural rhythm—a flow of messages back and forth between them. When one party is encoding ("sending") her message, the other party is decoding ("receiving") the code and translating it into a message. If both parties are sending, then neither party is likely to receive the message of the other. If both parties are receiving, there will be a period of unexpected silence. Most messages require a number of interchanges between the persons for the message to be understood. The following interview vignette illustrates a typical communication of one message from a client to her worker. Mrs. Cobb, a service worker, has been engaged with Mrs. N. for six weeks regarding medical problems of her eight-year-old son, Roy.

Worker: How's Roy doing, Mrs. N.?

Client: He's doing fine.

Worker: That's good to hear. The way you said that, it sounds as though something else is bothering you.

Client: Not really. Roy is all that matters. (Silence. Mrs. N.'s chin quivers; moisture forms in her eyes.) I'm ashamed. I guess I'm just tired of worrying, going from one problem to the next, never catching up. (Silence.)

Worker: You're pretty discouraged.

Client: Yeah. I missed work two days last week 'cause the sitter didn't show up. Now she says she's got a better job, and Roy still can't go back to school. If I have to quit my job I'll get so far behind again that I'll never catch up again.

Mrs. N.'s message to her worker was that, in spite of Roy's improved health, she was discouraged and worried about a sitter problem that might cause her to lose her job. As many messages are, this was a complex message conveyed in bits and pieces composed of ideas, emotions, and behaviors. To get the message accurately, the worker had to participate in a number of interchanges with the client, *listening carefully* with her *ears* and *eyes.* As she got pieces of the message, she fed back to the client what it seemed was being shared. The purpose of the feedback is to check the accuracy of the code being translated into the message. This allows the client either to correct what was misunderstood or to move further into the message. The rhythm of the communication is that of the worker's agreeing to listen actively, through various forms of verbal and nonverbal feedback, to the client's message as it is shaped in a variety of words, inflections, expressions, and gestures. At other times in the interview, when the worker has a message to send to the client, the same process in reverse must occur.

The code: a mixture of words, intonations, inflections, facial expressions, and gestures. There is an idea content to the message which the client sends. The ideas Mrs. N. expresses are: Roy's health is improved, my sitter didn't show up twice last week, I missed work those two days, my sitter has another job, Roy still can't go back to school. The message also has an emotional content to it: I'm ashamed (Roy's better so I ought to be happy, not sad), I'm discouraged (one problem right after another), I'm worried (I'll never catch up if I lose my job).

Ideas are conveyed primarily through words. Emotions are conveyed through voice tone and the way various words receive emphasis. In the illustration above, the client emphasized the word *he's* in her first response. The voice tone and the inflection cued the worker that Mrs. N. was upset. Her emotion was also conveyed through her facial expression, the quivering chin, and moistened eyes. First and foremost, the worker must hear the primary message Mrs. N. has to send about herself—essentially an emotional message. As noted earlier, empathy is the response of the worker that tunes in on that emotional message and communicates to the client that she has been heard and understood. The worker accomplishes this by a *reflection of feeling,* at one point saying "something else is bothering you," and again "you're pretty discouraged." In a reflection of feeling the worker identifies verbally the emotion it seems the client is expressing. Equally important, the worker expresses through her voice tones and inflection the emotion identified. This is done as briefly as possible as feedback to the client to check the accuracy of the perception.

Feedback of client ideas expressed is usually accomplished through a paraphrase. A paraphrase is putting the sender's ideas into one's own words. For instance, the worker could have responded to Mrs. N.'s remark, "He's doing fine," by saying, "He's not having any more trouble. That's good to hear. . . ." but chose to respond as she did because of the client's obvious "upsetness" which needed to be attended to. During the course of the interview, she must respond to the ideas of the client if appropriate problem-solving focus is to occur.

When using either a reflection of feeling or a paraphrase, the inflection of the worker should indicate tentativeness. The only way the worker can know that her perception is accurate is for the client to verify it through verbal and nonverbal feedback. For the worker to proceed without verification from the client presumes some level of omniscience on the worker's part, which could offend the client. In addition, a client may have mixed emotions and may not realize until she receives the feedback that what she has communicated is not what she intended. By inflecting the paraphrase or the reflection of feeling as a clarifying question, the worker prompts the client to correct any slight difference between what was heard and what was intended.

The code transmitting the message is not always consistent. In the discussion of genuineness, the importance of the worker's being congruent with herself is emphasized. One facet of congruence has to do with verbal and nonverbal codes fitting together to make a whole. If a person says, "I'm not sad," while at the same time his or her face is drawn tight and tears are forming, the person's words and nonverbal cues (parts of the code) don't match up. They appear to form a contradiction. Such contradictions lead to miscommunication. Whereas earlier we stressed worker behavior, now we need to be aware that clients don't always communicate congruently. The worker must take some responsibility for this problem if the interview is to be effective.

Contradictions between verbal and nonverbal cues, such as the one just mentioned, are a result of the client's emotional "upsetness." The contradiction may suggest that the client is unaware of the level of her sadness or that being sad is not acceptable to the client. A part of her simply will not allow the sadness to exist, although in fact it does. Each of us experiences these unconscious restraints or protections against painful emotions. Most contradictions in client communications reflect some level of the client's not facing up to a problem.

Occasionally, some contradictions result from the client's intentional effort to misrepresent the truth. Less politely stated, some clients sometimes lie. Just like the poker player who cannot keep a straight face when he bluffs, the person who lies frequently sends out nonverbal cues which suggest that the words do not accurately present the facts. It is best prevented by the worker's making clear to the client the importance of accuracy in information and precisely how the information will be used. In addition, where the information is for the purpose of determining the client's eligibility, the worker should point out that the application is a sworn statement and that the penalties for fraud are severe. Beyond this, a worker in the course of an *eligibility* interview should point out discrepancies or contradictions in the information received when they are recognized. Where contradictions occur in the course of *service* interviews the worker must make a judgment regarding the meaning of the contradiction, what it might possibly say about the client, and the usefulness to the client of pointing out the contradiction.

In the example of the lady who said she was not sad but had a drawn face and moisture in her eyes, the worker might have responded gently and with concern, "You look sad. You have tears in your eyes." In doing so the worker would have concluded that the client could have been led to face her sadness and with the support of the worker deal more directly with it. There are other times when this would have been inappropriate. This might have led to a level of intimacy inappropriate to the goals the client and the worker had agreed on. The worker might also consider it destructive at that point in the interview to take away from the client her defense of denial which kept her from experiencing the full impact of her sadness.

Pointing out contradictions in a client's words or between words and nonverbal behavior is called *confrontation.* A confrontation is not an accusation; rather, it is a verbal identification by the worker of ideas or ideas and emotions that are in conflict with each other. Having been presented with this information in a supportive fashion the client is enabled more fully to face the issue being avoided.

*The interview: dialogue and monologue.*We typically think of two person's talking to each other as a dialogue. Actually, each is carrying on a monologue in his or her head during the course of the dialogue (Kadushin, 1972: 38-40). What follows is a portion of an interaction between a caseworker and the mother of a six-year old child, Amy, in foster care. The mother, who abandoned the child three years ago, has come for one of her occasional, unannounced visits. The foster mother has called the caseworker to come to the home because the mother has Amy firmly in her grip and refuses to leave without her.

Dialogue	Monologue
Caseworker: Good morning Mrs. W. I am Amy's caseworker, Ms. C. It's good of you to come visit Amy.	Oh, my! Just look at Amy. she'll be upset for weeks. What kind of mother would do this to her child.

Client: I'm glad to meet you Mrs. C. Amy sure is glad to see me.

She looks young and inexperienced. I'm sure I can get her to let me take Amy with me.

Caseworker: Yes, Amy talks about you a lot. Just last week she asked how she could find you.

Mrs. W. seems frightened. She's really clinging to Amy. I've got to get her to calm down before she really gets Amy upset.

Client: Well, I'm planning to get married and move to Texas. Al is a wonderful man, says he'll take good care of Amy and me, and he does have a lot of money.

I gotta have this kid. That way Al will never leave me. . . . I got needs, too.

A careful study of this interchange reveals that three levels of messages are potentially present in any one piece of communication. Remembering that a piece of communication is made up of not only the words spoken but all of the nonverbal expressions as well, we note, first, that the speaker expresses something about herself. In the above illustration, the mother is expressing her own needs through her nonverbal behavior—clinging to the child—and through her comment that "Amy is glad to see me." Her message is, "Please, I need help as much as Amy does." The worker is saying that her primary concern is with the welfare of Amy. The child's well-being at the moment, as well as after the mother leaves, is upper-most in her mind. Second, each speaker expresses how she perceives the other—the mother perceives that the caseworker is young and inexperienced, a pushover. The worker perceives that the mother has great emotional needs obtained through Amy. The worker perceives that Amy is very vulnerable. Third, the speakers each are expressing a request of the other—the mother: "Hey, be a nice social worker, let me take Amy with me." The caseworker is requesting the mother to calm down. All of these communications occur in a matter of moments. Anytime I express myself I am: (1) saying something about myself—how I wish to be perceived, (2) saying something about the other person listening to me—how I perceive her; and (3) making a request of that person, which may be no more than, "Please listen to me." A competent caseworker is listening for all of these levels of the message. A part of her monologue sorts out implicit statements and questions. While we are not concerned here with the outcome of the case above, it is well to note that the competent worker will recognize and respond to the needs of the mother, as well as those of Amy, without jeopardizing the child's well-being or rights.

Language characteristics of a piece of communication are important. Every exchange in a dialogue can be examined regarding the focus of the remark and various qualitative dimensions. Focus is important since the theme of one person's comments often determines what the next person will say. The worker will not only pay close attention to the focus the client presents but also consider what the focus needs to be to more efficiently or effectively meet the client's needs. The focus in a sentence might be on the *client.* Such sentences made by the worker will include the client's name or the personal pronoun "you." If the client is focusing on herself the focus is usually manifested as an "I" statement. The focus may be on the *worker.* Here the worker makes an "I" statement, or the client focuses on the worker through the use of "you" or the worker's name. The focus may also be on the *worker-client* dyad. The theme in the sentence will allude to, or examine, their relationship or shared ideas, sometimes expressed as "we" statements. When the focus is on *others,* comments and expressions of feelings will be made about persons not present. The client with problems in interpersonal relationships frequently describes a problem by describing what someone else is doing to her. Sometimes the focus is on a *topic,* specifically examining an idea or piece of information such as food stamps or Work Incentive Program or other programs or services. There is a growing acceptance of the *cultural-environmental context* as the focus of problem solving. Here the person presents himself as a victim of a generalized or situational problem. Much is said today about the problems of the poor, the problems of elderly, the problems of women. Focusing on how "many elderly people have this same kind of problem" can relieve the client of undue worry about his or her own personal reactions to diminishing sight or hearing or other problems associated with aging.

Caseworkers will find that individual clients frequently will present the same themes over and over again. This may indicate how the client views herself, others, and the worker in relation to her problem. It is then very important for the worker to assess how much that particular focus facilitates or thwarts the problem resolution for the client.

Qualitative dimensions of communication. Several dimensions of communication can enhance the helping process. Those which relate to worker attributes have already been mentioned. Concreteness and immediacy are also important. Concreteness has to do with being specific. It is the opposite of vagueness.

> **Client:** I've been thinking about some things I could do to help my situation.

Here the client is vague and all inclusive in her comment. This kind of general comment cannot lead to problem solving and action that will lead to resolution. The client must be led to be more specific. The worker might respond:

> **Worker:** Good! Tell me what you've been thinking.
>
> **Client:** I thought I might ask my mother to come stay at my house until Roy is able to go back to school. But I'm afraid she'll ask me to move back home instead. So I don't like that idea. I also thought I might check with Happy Day Care Center and see if with a doctor's approval they might let me leave him there. I haven't called them yet, but thought I might.

Here the client is far more concrete. She expresses specific ideas (ask my mother . . . check with Happy Day . . .), and she expresses specific emotions (afraid she'll ask me to move home). The client describes the situation clearly as she perceives it and also outlines possible course of action. She will need additional assistance in putting her plans into actions; but concreteness is essential if any decision is to be made or any action is to be taken. Clients are not usually able to do this on their own; otherwise they would have already done so.

Immediacy has to do with whether the client is discussing her problem in terms of the past, the present, or the future. It's easy to dwell on the past, either how good or how bad it was. The past is rarely ever useful in problem solving except as it helps us to understand what we are doing in the present. The same is true of talking about what one is going to do "someday." Somehow someday never comes unless it is named and identified as a target date toward which actions are planned or upon which a specific action will be taken. The focus in problem solving is on now and the immediate future. Persons whose lives are full of pain and sadness may find it very difficult to give up the past or an undetermined future. Support and understanding matched with concreteness about the situation and the client's feeling can lead to slow but sure progress.

Language: a bridge or a block? Language should provide a bridge of communication between persons. Much of the time it does. At other times it seems that the harder we try to communicate, even with someone we want to communicate with, the more difficulty we have. Much of this is due to cultural and subcultural differences. Teenagers say they cannot talk to their parents. As a parent I may not like to admit it, but my fourteen, sixteen, and nineteen year olds belong to a different subcultural group than do my wife and I. They have different values (though I keep hoping not too different on fundamental matters), a different vocabulary, and different styles of communication (they communicate more indirectly through music, dance, and activities they can do side by side as well as together). At times it seems as if we have nothing in common except a roof and dining table.

Perhaps it is that we come at the same things in different ways. We just aren't on the same wavelength, so we find it hard to tune in on each other. As a parent this means that I must try harder if *I* want to communicate. I really don't get too upset about this. Actually, it's pretty healthy for my children to try out new perspectives, test out our family values, and see if they will stand the scrutiny of use.

When it comes to clients, caseworkers will find themselves dealing with a variety of different subcultural groups and major cultures as well. Over the United States, the majority of public welfare caseworkers are white, female, and middle class. Nearly all public welfare clients come from a lower socioeconomic group with substantially less education. Many are members of ethnic groups. Vocabulary and styles of communicating are very different. They form natural barriers. For instance, most white, middle-class persons consider looking at one another during the course of a conversation as a sign of openness and friendliness. However, among some blacks such eye contact is considered hostile. Among Latin Americans, where a male and female are in conversation such eye contact is considered seductive. The same behavior means different things in different cultures. Within the last few years the consciousness of Americans has been raised about the differences between the female and the male subcultures. It seems as though we've been operating as though there were only one group whose values counted.

Casework competence means appreciating differences in people. It means knowing your own values and how they push their way into your perceptions of right and wrong. It means knowing how to listen with your eyes and ears, being patient, and striving toward more precision in your own expressions of ideas and feelings. It means learning in every interview something new about the uniqueness of people and, where necessary, handling with great care the fragile expressions of other cultures or subculture groups.

Summary. Communication is an art and a skill. As a skill we know that when two people enter a dialogue, messages will flow back and forth clearly and accurately only if there is a rhythm established between the two so that while one is taking the part of the sender the other acts as the receiver of the sender's code. The receiver decodes the code and gives feedback to the sender to determine the accuracy of the reception. Several sequences or interchanges may occur, since the code is a complex arrangement of words, intonations, inflections, facial expressions, and gestures which are to some degree unique for each person. Sometimes there are contradictions in the code. Each individual in the dialogue carries on a monologue in his or her head, a part of which may deal with identified contradictions in verbal and nonverbal parts of the code in an attempt to make sense of them. Some apparent contradictions are really differences in vocabulary and styles of communication that result from the two persons in dialogue coming from either two different cultures or two different subcultural groups. Casework competence requires a high commitment to appreciating differences and making language a bridge of communication, rather than a barrier, between persons.

The interview: the roles are clearly defined. The interviewer is responsible for the interview. She is expected to know how to structure this formal conversation efficiently and effectively so that it meets the clients' goals. Obviously, knowing what needs to happen is not enough. The worker must also make what needs to happen occur: "make" not meaning to force but to engage the client with the same finesse and skill exhibited by a waitress with a tray loaded with food lifted high over her head weaving her way through a crowded restaurant. The waitress knows where she is going, anticipates the best route to get there, and is always prepared for the unexpected. In this regard, the role of the interviewee is to move in the direction pointed by the worker. The interviewee is a reactor—responding to the stimulus of the worker. The worker is not only a proactor—stimulating the client—but also a reactor, responding to the client, always with a view toward further stimulating the client toward her goal.

Sometimes these roles are reversed. The client takes the initiative and appears to be interviewing the worker: "Are you married? Do you have any children?" These inquiries are not usually based on idle curiosity. The client has a need to know more fully the kind of person she is trusting. She needs a sense of mutuality with the worker, a sense of the worker's humanity. She needs to verify through such questions that the two—worker and client—are more alike than different.

When interrogating a client who has a material need that the caseworker cannot meet, the client's manner may be hostile. The emotional tone is angry with undertones of resentment. This kind of role reversal easily puts the caseworker on the defensive—an expected human reaction but not a very professional response. Another form of role reversal which has some hostile overtones is seen in the questioning of the worker's performance or follow-through on a client service.

> **Worker**: I know we talked about getting an appointment for you for an eye examination, but I haven't got to it yet. I'm sorry, and I'll try to get it done soon.
>
> **Client**: Why's it taking so long? My eyes are really bothering me. Can't you call now?

The hostile overtones here are associated with appropriate anger at the worker for not following through as promised. The worker may have had good reasons. But the vagueness of her statement doesn't indicate what those reasons are and adds to the client's irritation. The following more specific or concrete explanation would have been more effective in maintaining a positive working relationship with this client:

> **Worker**: When I promised you I would get an appointment for you I misjudged how many clients I would have come in this week. I have a number of appointments I have not been able to get set up. Yours is one of them. I have scheduled the time this afternoon to handle them. I'm sorry about the delay.
>
> **Client**: My eyes are really bothering me. Can't you call now?

The worker's response to the last question will depend on whether the appropriate people to call are available and whether the client's behavior is judged as hostile manipulation or genuine distress over her eyes. Hostile manipulation is best handled in a matter-of-fact and straightforward manner.

> **Worker:** You seem pretty irritated at me about this.
>
> **Client:** Naw, my eyes just hurt me.
>
> **Worker:** They're bothering you a great deal, aren't they? I'm really sorry, but I need to call when I can handle all appointments at one time. Since I've set aside the time, I am sure I will have it done this afternoon. Can you call in the morning for the information?

It may be argued that setting limits with clients such as this impairs a positive relationship. This could be true if there were not a tone and feeling of warmth and concern in the worker's voice as she replies. But being clear about what can be done reasonably and sticking with it *unless there is a sense of crisis in the air* is important if the client is to respect the worker. On the other hand, respect will not be forthcoming if the worker doesn't follow through in the afternoon and have the information available the following morning.

Phases of the interview. An interview has a beginning, a middle, and an end. When you think about it, most conversations have those same three parts. Usually there is a brief greeting, a large body of discussion, and a brief good-by. Each of these three parts has a particular function in a casework interview.

The introductory phase: getting acquainted and agreeing about the purpose of the interview. Both client and worker, on first meeting, are sizing each other up. One client wrote of her expectations of the social worker she would meet, "I had visions of a rigid, forbidding type of person. . . . I was informed by friends that social workers asked humilating questions, examined the closets, and inspected the bed linen."[1] As she meets the worker, however, we'll hope she's pleasantly surprised to find a warm, genuinely caring, empathic person. She'll be comparing the worker with the model in her head. It's also probable that she'll be trying to put her best foot forward, making every effort to make a good impression. So she'll be anxious. The worker, on the other hand, probably has had more contact with clients than the client has had with workers. She should be more relaxed because of her experience, but this may not be the case. This may be her first client since joining the agency. As the worker greets the client, the brief period of welcome is quite similar to a social occasion, a visit of a friend to one's home.

You, the worker want, to make the client feel welcome. You may need to help her with her coat. You want her to adjust to the surroundings; you want her to be comfortable with you. A few moments, maybe less than two minutes, of small talk will accomplish this. Talk about the weather, the traffic, anything that's not personal or demanding on the client. I keep a pitcher of water and paper cups on my table. I like to offer a drink of water as a gesture of welcome and caring. Most clients gladly accept. It's something concrete, refreshing, and appropriate to any client. At this point you are interested in making an appropriate impression on the client. You want the client to see you as competent (in control of the interview), warm (a smile makes a big difference), and understanding (helping her feel at ease gets this across). You are also interested in sizing up this client. As you interact, you will notice her dress, her facial expression, the firmness of her grip as you shake her hand, the volume and tone of her speech, anything about the client that may be a clue to better understanding her, and, in particular, her mood and frame of mind as she enters the interview. You will notice how well she is able to relax as you go through the ritual of welcome. Not being able to relax is a possible sign that this client is under significant stress unrelated to the interview setting.

Names are important. Getting names clear is important from the outset. The Biblical injunction against taking the Lord's name in vain is aimed not at cursing but at being *careless* with the name of God. A person's name in a real sense is his being; it's who he is. Look me in the eye and call me by name correctly and you make me know I am important to you. This is a significant and essential early step in relationship formation. Some names are difficult, so being careful with a person's name may mean asking how to pronounce it. If my name's not important to you, then probably I am not either. Be equally sure that your client gets your name clear. She will thus feel more personally connected to you.

In the beginning, it's important to use titles. Mr., Mrs., and Miss lend a sense of formality appropriate to the setting. They are marks of respect. Over time in a service relationship, probably more than in an eligibility relationship, it may become appropriate for both client and caseworker to use first names. In such cases, the dropping of the title represents a more intimate relationship, which could facilitate providing the service to the client. Under no circumstances should the caseworker call the client by her first name without the understanding with the client that she is to do likewise. If the client is not comfortable with this, then the worker should also stay with the title. Titles really don't get in the way of developing an effective, helping relationship.

Clients need help in feeling important. Since many county departments operate on an "open door" policy, clients may wait to see their caseworkers longer than they had anticipated. Even though this inconvenience is not the fault of the caseworker and is a result of a policy designed to meet many low-income persons' need to come when they can get to the department, it is appropriate and hospitable for the worker to acknowledge with regret the delay. Such a courtesy, as the interview gets under way, lets the client know that the worker was aware of her even before she greeted her, again adding to her sense of importance.

Just a word about adding to your client's "sense of importance." As mentioned earlier, most public welfare clients have a pretty low opinion of themselves—frequently termed "low self-esteem." This is a major aspect of the client's frequent lack of motive. Anything the worker can do to increase the client's sense of self-worth increases the chances of the client's coping with and resolving problems. In this instance, improved self-esteem results as the client catches a glimpse of herself in the worker's eye and is encouraged by what she sees and feels. What a marvelous contribution to make to a person on an occasional day in his or her life!

Identify the purpose of the interview. Beyond the getting acquainted and getting settled that is accomplished in the first few minutes of the interview, the introductory phase addresses the reason for the client's visit to the agency. She has a purpose, or she has come at the request of the worker; the reason needs to be identified. Unless the worker has solicited the client's presence and therefore knows the purpose, it is well to move into this part of the interview with a "structured open question." Example: "What is it that you wanted to see me about today?" This is an open question, since it allows the client to say in as many words as she chooses whatever is on her mind. But the open question is structured by the caseworker's focus on the client's purpose in coming to the interview. It is therefore preferable to an unstructured open question such as "How are things going?" This added structure is very important. Not only does it get the interview focused on professional business as a transition from hosting courtesies, but it also assists the client in organizing her presentation of her problem situation or need. The client doesn't have to play a guessing game about what's expected, what the caseworker needs to know. Such structured questions are like clearly marked road signs, "Next right, Savannah." What a relief to see that sign when I'm uncertain where to turn! The competent caseworker will consistently point the way while leaving plenty of latitude for the client to drive the car.

The introductory phase concludes as the client and the caseworker identify and agree on the purpose of the interview. In some instances this may take quite awhile. The client may have a number of problems and need to touch on several of them before deciding which needs to be addressed on this particular day and which can wait until later. This exploration is helped along by a group of "attending skills," so called because they communicate to the client that she has the full attention of the worker, who earnestly wants to know what's troubling her.

Attending skills include nonverbal behavior on the part of the worker. The worker needs to be *relaxed* herself. This means being comfortable, but not slouched, in your chair. Sit facing the client, if possible without a desk directly between the two of you. As the client talks maintain steady (but not staring) eye contact, keep your facial expression alive (not frozen in a smile or solemn expression). Verbal responses useful in helping the client explore are: open questions, structured open questions, minimal encouragers, reflections of feeling, paraphrases, and interpretations. Except for minimal encouragers and interpretations, each of these responses has been defined earlier.

The less verbal client. Brief verbal responses of one or two words, along with nonverbal signals such as positive head nods, fall in the category of "minimal encouragers." By looking (not staring) at the client's eyes—even if the client is looking away—nodding your head, and slightly smiling as you say, "Uh huh," "yes," "Please go on," or repeating the last one or two words or a phrase spoken by the client, you communicate your attention as well as your desire for the client to continue talking. With clients who appear to be somewhat "nonverbal" and may in fact have considerable difficulty in putting their thoughts into words, clients who feel self-conscious and shy in the interview setting, this kind of encouragement can make a great deal of difference. Just getting this client to talk about anything may be a major step for her in developing a new skill in coping.

When a caseworker uses minimal encouragers as described above, he is applying an important principle—postive reinforcement—to change a person's behavior. Briefly, this means that the caseworker identifies in his mind exactly what he wants the client to do, and, as soon as the client does it, the caseworker immediately rewards her appropriately. In the case of the client who sits silently, what the caseworker identifies in his head as desired is for the client to speak. At this point it is not *what* the client says as much as the client's *act of speaking* that has been identified as needed. So as soon as the client says a word the caseworker rewards the word with a nod and a smile. If the client pauses, the caseworker offers a one- or two-word response to signal his desire for the client to continue.

If the one- or two-word response is not enough to keep the client talking, then a further, positively reinforcing response may be offered, identifying the desired behavior in a complimentary fashion: "I really appreciate what you just said; that helps me to understand; please tell me more," followed by good eye contact, a gentle smile, and a look of expectancy.

The important thing to remember about positive reinforcement is that you avoid the natural inclination to tell a person what he or she is doing wrong. That kind of criticism is easy but only reminds the person of undesired behavior and, in the case of the reticent client, makes her even more conscious of her inability to speak easily. Instead of identifying the undesired behavior, the caseworker silently asks herself, "What is the opposite behavior from the one I don't want?" Having answered that question, the caseworker watches for the desired behavior, and, as soon as it occurs, responds affirmatively, warmly rewarding the client's action and reinforcing it, making the client aware of her ability to do what she probably finds very difficult. Positive reinforcement has an application in many other aspects of casework and also areas of personal living such as child management.

Interpretation. As noted earlier, interpretation is another caseworker response that assists the client in determining the primary purpose or focus of the interview. Interpretation is any verbal response by the caseworker that takes the facts, ideas, or feelings presented by a client and puts them into a new frame of reference. For instance:

> **Client** (who has a record of absenteeism): Gee, I wish I didn't miss so much work!
>
> **Worker**: You've been absent from work an awful lot and you know how bosses feel about that, so you wonder what's going to happen to you now.

An interpretation is different from a   paraphrase or a reflection of feeling. Each of these picks up on ideas or emotions and, as simply and accurately as possible, restates those ideas or emotions for the client. Notice the examples below:

> **Client** (who has a record of absenteeism): Gee, I wish I didn't miss so much work!
>
> **Worker**: You're pretty upset and worried about this (*reflection of feeling*).

or

> **Worker**: You've been missing work lately (*paraphrase*).

The interpretation combines both the feelings and the emotions of the client in the caseworker's response and *adds* the worker's point of view on their meaning or significance to the client. Clients do not always accept the worker's interpretation as their own and may even reject it entirely. But the function of the interpretation is frequently simply to make the client take a position on her own point of view with definite movement toward deciding the purpose of the interview. Reflections of feeling and paraphrases tend to generate in the client an awareness that the caseworker understands what's being said. They also allow the client to explore more fully the feeling or feelings being experienced or ideas being considered—without adding an outside dimension from the worker.

The skillful use of closed and structured open questions funnels the client's thinking toward a purpose. Clearly stated structured open questions and closed questions help the client to make decisions about what is important and what is not important. Such questions narrow or limit the discussion.

> **Worker:** Is keeping this job the most important thing on your mind today?
>
> **Client:** Yes, it sure is.
>
> **Worker:** Let's think about that then. How close to losing the job are you?

Notice that the worker has used a closed question that required the client to make a decision or a value judgment about her work. The closed question is immediately followed by a structured open question that allows the client freedom to express her feelings about one aspect of losing her job, the time frame. Had the client answered "no" to the closed question, the worker could have followed with a different structured open question, "What is?," again requiring the client to make a decision regarding the purpose of the interview.

Please note that I have avoided suggesting that the client be asked the question "Why?" I strongly suggest you remove that word from your professional vocabulary. I have removed it from mine. The reason is simple. Instead of being heard as a neutral inquiry about the cause or reason for something, the majority of the time it is heard as disapproval or displeasure. It communicates to the client that she has done something "wrong" or that she has behaved "badly." The way the worker asks "why" really does not matter. Our culture has conditioned the client to respond negatively and defensively. Only little children seem able to ask "why?" (regarding the mysteries around them) without implying a moral judgment; and even they soon learn to ask the question as an expression of disapproval ("Why'd you give him that piece of cake?"). It is no surprise that the typical response to "Why?" is "Because." Since your client will undoubtedly misunderstand your meaning, I suggest you substitute the word "what" in its place. Instead of "Why were you not at home for our appointment?" one could say, "What kept you from being home for our appointment?" Besides avoiding the negative magic of "Why?" the use of "What?" carries an automatic positive value, implying that the speaker assumes there was a reason or something which prevented the client from being at home. Rather than sounding like an accusation of wrongdoing, it sounds like an effort to understand. I've made my case, but you can check it out the next time someone asks you "Why?" See how you respond. Defensively, I'll bet (Benjamin, 1969: 197).

The development phase explores the problem in depth. Most of the interview time should be spent in exploring in-depth the focus agreed on with the client. Having reached agreement, it is the responsibility of the caseworker to assist the client in examining every significant aspect related to this purpose. This portion of the interview should be an experience for the client and the worker similar to that of a jeweler's slowly turning a diamond as it is examined under a microscope. As light is allowed to fall on each facet of the gem, the eye is filled with a variety of colors and tones. Each is a mirror, reflecting through the light the very character of the stone. In much the same way the caseworker keeps the client's attention on the topic by slowly uncovering with the client her understanding of the matter in question, her emotional involvement, how the various aspects of the problem affect each other, how she and others are involved, and what alternatives are available.

During this part of the interview the client should be assisted to face her dilemma and to express out loud, for herself as well as the worker to hear, whatever she feels or thinks, no matter how painful to hear. When Mrs. S., describing the recent loss of her eight-year-old son by pneumonia, said, "I let him die! I couldn't pay for the medicine when he needed it! I didn't give him enough food! I kept him in that sticking hole until it was too late," the urge to say "It's not really your fault" is held back as both the client and the caseworker experience guilt for the death of a defenseless child. Hurting with her, the caseworker responds, "You feel guilty and angry that you could do so little." And the client digs deeper, since the worker does not stand in the way of her confronting how much she hates herself and others for allowing her child to die. "Yes! Nobody did anything—until it was too late." As she weeps, the moisture in the worker's eyes expresses the nagging pain inside. "Oh, how I miss him," she says. "He's gone." The worker's willingness to walk in the "valley of the shadow of death" with her client, bearing with her the pain of loss, makes it possible for her to face and to survive the full reality of her child's death.

This interview might explore other aspects of the client's life as a result of the child's death—such as unexpected expenses related to the funeral, disposition of the child's clothing, toys, and other personal items, how the other children are managing, and budget adjustments (yes, even that) brought on by the reduction in AFDC for a family of five instead of six.

The worker will find that the client will bring in many matters only slightly related to the central purpose of the interview. Since it is the responsibility of the worker to keep the two on target, she must use a technique called "selective attention" to draw the client back to the agreed-upon focus. For instance:

> **Client** (discussing problem in securing child care): I've looked at a lot of day care centers. Not many of them do anything to teach the kid. When I was a child my mother said the lady that kept me had me saying my ABCs by the time I was three. I still see that lady, and every time I do I tell her how much I appreciate the good start she gave me. She is eighty-five years old and in poor health now. I feel like I owe her something, ought to visit with her, do something for her.
>
> **Worker** (selectively attending to the portion of the conversation related to the purpose—day care): You want a day care center with an educational program and you haven't found one yet.

The worker has ignored the client's comments about her friend, not because they were not meaningful to the client but because the client had inadvertently spun herself off into a topic not immediately related to the purpose of the interview. Sometimes the worker has to be more direct by saying, "We need to get back to your concern for good day care" or "how does what you were just saying fit with your concern for good day care?" When the purpose of the interview has been accomplished, or when time runs out, or when the client and the worker agree that no more can be accomplished on a given day, the interview moves toward the ending or closing phase.

The transition from the developmental to the ending phase should be clearly recognized both by client and worker. Moving into closing phase is not always easy. The client may not be ready to leave. The caseworker may feel uneasy about the client and unwilling to let her go. But endings must come, and just as the beginning of the interview is planned to move the client into the main purpose of the contact, so the ending phase is planned to move the client out of the contact. The caseworker must alert the client to this transition.

The most effective way to initiate the transition is to summarize briefly what has been covered, accomplished, or agreed on during the course of the interview. Such a summary may pick up on the themes discussed in the particular focus or purpose of the interview and allow the client to react to the overall picture.

> **Worker**: Let's see now, we wanted to explore your job situation. You decided you were not about to get fired even though you've been absent a lot. But you think you need to talk to your supervisor and let her know you want to do better. You figured your child care is a big reason for your absences and have decided to locate a day care center in place of your present sitter. Is that pretty much where we've come today? What have I missed?
>
> **Client**: That's about it. I'm really glad you helped me decide to talk to my supervisor. It's always been easier to avoid her.
>
> **Worker**: You've made a tough but important decision. I think you're taking the right steps. Give me a call later this week and let me know how that works out. . . . Next time let's work on the day care problem if you haven't worked it out by then.

The client is well aware that the interview is concluding. She has given her impression about what has been done and related her decision to an upcoming action. The worker has *linked the interview* to what the client will do by asking for feedback: "Give me a call." This assures the client of the worker's genuine interest, but more importantly it maintains the "presence" of the worker with the client as she makes contact with the supervisor. She is more likely to follow through since she and the caseworker have an understanding that she will check back. Notice also that the caseworker links this interview purpose to a likely focus for their next contact. But by saying "If you haven't worked it out by then," the worker lets the client know that her help is available but that she is confident the client can act on her own.

The closing is marked by a gradual reduction in emotion-filled discussion and a focus on the positive image of the client. Plans for future contact are made. As in the beginning, some light conversation about the ordinary business of living—the weather, the traffic, whatever is unrelated to current issues in the person's life—helps with the transition out of the interview.

The caseworker's purpose often determines the kind of interview. Interviews are generally one of three kinds—diagnostic, informational, or therapeutic. When a person such as the client above, requests help with a problem regarding job performance, the worker may decide she needs a good deal of new information about how the client has performed in other work settings and in organizations to which she has belonged. This is usually structured into a WIN interview. Here the worker is doing a social study—gathering information on how well the client interacts with people in accomplishing a task. The caseworker's concern is the client's social functioning. This information is needed if the client is to be understood and assisted in the problem-solving process.

Other interviews are aimed at appraisal or determination. These are decision-making interviews for the caseworker. Here the worker must get selected information, usually that required by the agency, to determine the eligibility or appropriateness of the client for the agency service. As in AFDC and foodstamp applications, specific information is required.

The therapeutic interview reflects a careful and deliberate effort toward resolving a dilemma in the client's life. Here the worker is trying to assist the client toward more effective social functioning, an improvement in the way she deals with people in accomplishing tasks and goes about meeting her own needs and the needs of those for whom she is responsible. More attention will be given to this kind of interview in the problem-solving section.

Exercises

The following statements by a worker were made during various parts of an interview. In the blank beside each, identify the phase of the interview (introductory, developmental, or ending) in which you think the statement was made. On the lines beneath each statement explain your reason for choosing the phase you did.

_____ Let me see if I understand you; you've had a lot of trouble with your back lately, you've missed a lot of work, and your kids have been sick. But the reason you came in today was to get some help for your son?

_____

_____

_____ I know you had a hard time getting here in the traffic today.

I sure hope it won't be that difficult on the way home.

_____

_____

——————— I don't think I fully understand your problem with Joe.
Please say some more about how you get upset.

_____

_____

Write below a brief exchange you have recently had with a client. Write beside each verbal expression the monologue that you were carrying on in your head and what you speculate the client was saying to herself as well.

Dialogue	Monologue
Worker:	
_____	_____
_____	_____
Client:	
_____	_____
_____	_____
Worker:	
_____	_____
_____	_____
Client:	
_____	_____

Thinking about the three levels of messages in the above exchange, identify:

(1) what the speakers were saying about themselves _____

_____

_____

_____

(2) what the speakers were saying about the other person _____

_____

_____

(3) what the speakers are requesting of the other person _____

_____

_____

_____

5

TASK-FOCUSED PROBLEM SOLVING

As previously noted, effective and efficient use of an interview is an essential part of good social work technique. The social worker's use of the interview is very much like the carpenter's use of his tools of trade. The skilled carpenter must be able to saw and nail together various materials with precision. But if he is to make anything—a cabinet or a house—he must have a plan, an overall design which directs his skills toward a desired goal. The same is true with a social worker. His skills must be directed by an overall plan, a method to guide him in applying his skills systematically.

This section outlines one such guide, task-focused problem solving. It has been selected because of its effective use by public welfare workers. The model as presented here is an adaptation of William Reid and Laura Epstein's *Task-Centered Casework* (1972). Much of the modification grows out of my experience in using Helen Harris Perlman's (1979) problem-solving approach to casework.

The professional helping relationship as previously described is the foundation for this approach. Empathy, warmth-respect, and genuineness enable the client and worker to engage in the process that will bring about or lead toward a solution for the client's problem situation. The quality of the helping relationship is essential. Any effort to apply the following guidelines without regard to this fundamental aspect is likely to fail. If you haven't read the first sections of this book, I urge you to read them now before continuing this chapter.

Casework is directed toward either establishing a client's eligibility for a program or service or assisting a client in resolving problems in living. Eligibility casework is gaining the necessary information from the client to make an accurate determination. A moderate use of the core helping conditions while completing the necessary forms is usually sufficient to communicate to the client the interest and concern of the worker and to provide the worker an adequate opportunity to identify client problems requiring a referral to a service caseworker. Task-focused problem solving is an approach that will guide the service caseworker in helping clients resolve problems in living.

Problem solving is not solution giving. Most of us have had problems growing out of: (1) the purchase of merchandise that we discovered was defective; or (2) attempting to resolve a problem with someone with whom we live or work. So we say to a friend, "I don't know what I'm going to do, I've taken my car back to the garage five times and it still doesn't run right." And the friend, wishing to be helpful, responds, "Why don't you call the Better Business Bureau?" Or we say, "I sure dread the weekends. All that washing and house cleaning and I can't get my husband to lift a finger!" The friend responds, "That wouldn't happen to me. Just leave his clothes and wash your own." The problem statement each time meets with a piece of advice, a solution. Your client probably has had very similar experiences with neighbors, friends, and relatives who mean well but who do not know how to help the client solver her problem. For a variety of reasons, the solutions which have been offered simply do not work for the client.

Solutions must be personalized. Calling the Better Business Bureau may have been what my friend used as a solution when he had a car repair problem, and perhaps it worked for him. But he does not know that I refused the mechanic's advice that I allow him to replace my carburetor with a new one and instead had him repair the old one. In the other instance, my friend may gain her husband's cooperation by ignoring his needs, a perfectly appropriate course of action within the values or rules of her family. She does not know that in my family such behavior would be considered childish and would cause me to lose the respect of husband and children. The solutions to a person's problems must grow out of her values, must be within her abilities to put them into practice, and must fit her unique problem situation. Task-focused problem solving assumes that the worker's responsibility is: (1) to enable the client to identify *the* problem or problems which need to be solved; (2) to enable the client to formulate the actions which must be taken to resolve each problem; and (3) to enable the client to put into practice the actions that have been formulated. Emphasis is on the client's resolving her own problems through caseworker assistance.

The task-focused problem-solving approach. The task approach begins with the caseworker's explaining in the first interview how she can help the client, what her role is, and what the client's role is in the helping process. If the client has come by way of a referral, the worker clearly states the reason for the referral: "Mrs. Carter, your AFDC caseworker said you were having some problems with your children's school." Having briefly outlined the task-focused problem-solving approach the worker proceeds to the next step, problem exploration. After the client has identified the problems confronting her, she is assisted in coming to an agreement with the worker on one or two *target* problems on which they will work. The client describes what she wants in the way of change to resolve the target problems. These are listed as the specific or general goals of the client and caseworker. Next, each target problem is analyzed carefully. Then an appropriate task (or tasks) for the client is formulated, and actions required by the caseworker on behalf of the client are identified. The client is then rehearsed in the performance of the task or tasks. Future interviews evaluate the client's success in carrying out the tasks and modify or redesign the tasks. At some point in the first or second interview--most frequently at the point of identifying the target problem—a contract, either verbal or in writing, is agreed on. It should state briefly each target problem, the goal described by the client, and the frequency and number of interviews the worker and the client will have to work on the target problem. Each of these steps will now be considered in detail.

Explaining the process to the client. From the outset, the client needs to know what will happen to her in the problem-solving process. Even though a client may be coming at the suggestion of an eligibility worker or a colleague from another agency, she needs to hear the worker state her understanding of the referral. At the conclusion of the explanation, the worker will ask for feedback from the client about the accuracy of her understanding of the general referral purpose. It is not unusual for the client to state that the problem is a little different from the one suggested by the referral source. Frequently, the referral explanation given by another social worker or by a member of the client's family reflects how that person sees the client's problem rather than how the client sees her need. Knowing how someone else views the client is important in understanding better the client's contacts in her social environment. The worker begins the first interview with a statement of the reason for referral to relieve the client of as much anxiety as possible about what her new caseworker knows and thinks about her. Having *briefly* established how the referral came about, the worker gives a brief explanation of the helping process.

> **Worker:** I'm glad you've come in. Let me tell you how I can be of help. Today I'd like to get a better understanding of your situation, identify any other problems that may be causing difficulty, and be sure we are going to work on the problem most important to you. When we've come to an agreement on that problem, it becomes our target. We'll next decide what changes you want made in order to resolve the target problem. We then begin to think about what you and I can do about this target problem. We may not get that figured out today, but by the end of our second interview we should have something we're doing about the problem. We'll decide at that time how many more interviews we will work together on the target

problem and how frequently we'll need to have contact. We want to get some relief for you as soon as possible. Now, let's see what questions you have about how we will work together.

The road map has been laid out. No doubt the client has only limited comprehension of what will actually happen, but she has a glimpse. If she has no questions at this point, she at least has something which she has heard and which she can clarify later if needed. At the least, she gets a sense that the caseworker knows what she is doing, that she is competent to help. This impression is crucial in problem solving. When the client comes to the interview on her own initiative rather than by referral from another professional, the worker moves directly from the welcoming portion of the interview to this brief explanation.

*Problem exploration.*Getting a sense of the client's world as she sees it is necessary if the caseworker is to participate fully in problem solving. No one's life is simple. No problem stands alone. Each is always interconnected with other problems. A variety of circumstances and people will make even those problems that appear similar unique. The caseworker must now lead the client in an exploration of her world. This may be quite painful for the client and the worker. As indicated earlier in the section on the interview, "attending skills," including open questions, structured open questions, minimal encouragers, reflections of feeling, paraphrases, and interpretations greatly assist the client to explore her view of her circumstances. The caseworker attempts to broaden the client's point of view while not introducing anything new or unrelated to the client's presentation.

The client will likely cover many problematic areas. As the discussion continues it may become apparent that the client is more concerned about a problem other than the one she cited at the beginning of the interview. This should be no surprise. It's often hard for a person to come right out and say what's bothering her. The caseworker is cued to the importance of a problem by the amount of emotion that the client expresses as the topic is discussed. Speech may become more rapid or dramatically slowed. Voice intonation may change significantly. The client's facial expression and body posture may reflect tensed muscles. Clothing may show perspiration even though the room is cool.

As the problem exploration proceeds, the caseworker carries on a monologue in her head. "Is this problem more important than any other the client has noted? How is this problem connected to the others? What has this problem in common with the other problems mentioned?" The caseworker is attempting to make a tentative judgment about what problem should be addressed. Essentially, the worker is trying to assign an order of priority or importance to the problems the client lists. In reporting her conclusions to the client, she might say, "As I've listened to you it sounds like you are most concerned about child care during your stay at the hospital. Other concerns are your worries about the surgery, added medical expenses, and how you'll manage the house while you are recuperating after surgery. But the big thing right now seems to be getting child care arrangements worked out. How do you see it?" If the client agrees with the caseworker's assessment and states her willingness to work on the problem, the exploration phase is over.

Selecting, agreeing on, and committing to work on *one* problem doesn't mean that the client is left with no help with the other problems. It does mean that the energy of both the caseworker and the client will be concentrated on the most important issue in the client's life right now, as determined by the client. That's important to remember in this approach. In the example above, the caseworker might have considered it more important to begin to prepare the client for her surgery by working through her feelings of anxiety and fear. The client's judgment, however, takes precedence. The worker's role is to clarify sufficiently the client's mixed emotions and confused ideas so that the client can see clearly what she values and most immediately needs.

Sometimes more than one problem can be worked on at a time. This can occur when there is great similarity between two problems, as in the illustration above. The client is concerned about child care during her hospital stay and about homemaker or home health care services after she returns home to recuperate. It's possible that the worker may consider these sufficiently similar to suggest that the client have a two-prong target. This is a matter of judgment based on knowledge of services in the community. Even when similar to the primary target, the second should not be added unless the worker considers that the client is as likely to succeed with the two as with the one. Where there is doubt, the worker should suggest the second problem be taken up after the first has been resolved. Other problems may follow as well.

When the target problem has been agreed on and committed to, the first part of the "contract" has been completed. The target problem is then translated into the desired or needed *goal* for problem resolution. The caseworker next suggests a specific time within which the two will work together on resolving the target problem. This is spelled out in numbers of interviews rather than dates. Frequency of interviews will also be discussed. The time factor will vary with the nature of the problem, as few as one additional contact or as many as twelve. Under some circumstances the interviews may occur weekly. But sometimes seeing the client two or more times during the week may be more appropriate. Crisis situations, as considered in the next chapter, frequently require more contacts within a brief length of time than do chronic problems of long-standing distress.

Time is critical. Deadlines tend to mobilize a person's energy. Some individuals put off until the last minute very important or difficult tasks, partly because the task is approached with dread but partly because the person knows "when *I have to,* I can get it done!" This approach uses time as a facilitator of actions toward a solution.

Since the caseworker has specified how many interviews she will work with the client on the target problem, the passing of each interview marks the reduction of a significant resource— the caseworker's expertise and energy. (Don't laugh. You've got a lot to offer the client; recognize it and use it). The client's sense of the caseworker's enthusiasm, care, concern, and competence will add importance to the casework relationship beyond the anticipated relief that problem resolution promises.

Another important aspect of using time in problem-solving is that in most casework the greatest amount of progress toward resolution is made very soon after the client solicits the caseworker's help. As a result, the discomfort that usually comes with a problem is greatly reduced soon after casework begins, even though the problem may not have been resolved. Usually the discomfort is lessened by the client's adjusting to or accepting things as they are or feeling more secure in her situation with the caseworker's support. Knowing this, the caseworker attempts to get the client moving while the motivating discomfort is still high. To take advantage of the time factor, problem exploration must be completed no later than the conclusion of the second interview—and preferably within the first interview. Thus the caseworker's problem-solving process makes use of nature's own problem solving process.

Now describe the goal. The flip side of any problem is its solution. The client will have an idea of how things would be if the target problem were resolved. This goal should be clearly defined so that both the caseworker and the client understand what they are working toward. Otherwise, each may have a different idea of what is expected. Also, it's extremely important for both to be able to recognize when the target problem has been resolved. Example:

> **Target problem:** Mrs. J. can't get Joe, her son, to come home at night.
> **Goal:** Joe will be home each night by nine o'clock.

The client has described clearly how things will be when the target problem is resolved. She has stated her goal with regard to the target problem. Such goal statements are consistent with Title XX expectations for public welfare casework.

The contract: oral or written? Having identified the target problem and the goal the client expects as a result of the work with the caseworker, the worker decides how often the client contact will occur. Both the number and frequency of the contacts is discussed until agreement is reached. Finally, the worker states the contract—the understanding agreed on, including the target problem, goal, and time period in which the casework is to be done. Whether placed in writing or left as an oral statement, this understanding is the contract which binds worker and client together in this problem-solving effort. It stands as the "landmark" for this series of casework contact—a point of understanding to which either client or worker can refer back as the need arises. Example:

> Contract: Mrs. J. can't get Joe, her son, to come home. She wants him home each night by nine o'clock. We will work toward this goal for ten to twelve weeks, meeting approximately twelve times.

*Problem analysis comes next.*The range of problems has been explored and placed into the client's order of importance. A target problem has been identified. (On some occasions two targets are selected.) A contract has been reached between the worker and the client that states either orally or in writing the target problem, the goal, the number of interviews to be used, and the frequency of interviews and telephone contacts. Next, the target problem must be thoroughly analyzed.

Whereas in problem exploration the client is encouraged to touch on all those features of her current life situation which are problematic, the worker now structures her questions to remain on the target problem. The worker and the client need to understand what causes the problem. Questions which focus on this facet of the problem situation might be: "What do you think has brought (the target problem) about?" or "Who do you think has brought this situation about?" or "What part do you play in making (the target problem) occur?" Obviously some problems, such as the lady's needing child care while she is in the hospital, have very clear causes. The cause for her problem is her poor health. Other causes might relate to her having no mate, no family who will offer to help, or no neighbors who are close friends. Other problems may have far more complex causes that will not be altogether clear even after careful examination. Emotional upset where there is no situational dilemma is one such problem area. These problems are usually referred to professionals with specialized training—the clinical social worker in a mental health center, a psychiatrist, or a psychologist.

In addition to understanding as much as possible the cause or causes—not only the part other people play in the problem but also the part the client plays—the worker will lead the client to examine her emotional response and involvement in the problem. What personal meaning does the client attach to the problem? What does she believe about herself in relation to the problem? What does she believe about others? What effect does it have on her? From her beliefs flow her emotions and her actions. The client needs to have as good a sense of this area as she can. Emotional involvement sometimes means the client is overreacting, seeing the problem as far more serious or urgent than it is. The client may be so sensitive in the problem area that she adds to her problem by reacting defensively or aggressively toward people who might be a resource, or a part of a solution.

The worker can assist the client in becoming more aware of her emotional involvement by giving accurate feedback. For example:

> **Worker:** As I listed to you talk about your neighbor helping you out it seemed to me there was a bit of anger in your voice.
>
> **Client:** I guess so. She knows I've got to find somebody. I've helped her enough. You'd think she'd offer.

or

> **Worker:** Do you realize that every time we start talking about your children coming back home you get very quiet?
>
> **Client:** I guess I'm afraid I'll lose them again.

Other forms of feedback, which can heighten the client's awareness of emotional involvement, are as follows: *noting repetitions,* statements which the client seems to come back to in the interview; *identifying* for the client *physical behavior* that suggests anxiety ("You were really fidgeting in your chair as you were talking, does that mean that's too personal to talk about?"). *A word of caution:* feedback must be accompanied with a high level of warmth-respect; otherwise the client's anxiety will increase and she will become defensive. This would of course defeat the purpose of feedback—to increase client self-awareness.

As the client is digging deeper into the various parts of the target problem that the worker is carrying on in her head, a monologue different from that conducted during the problem exploration. Now the worker is making mental notes regarding possible actions (tasks) the client may take in resolving her problem. As the client mentions her neighbor as an unlikely prospect for help, the worker wonders to herself, "What keeps her from asking her neighbor? What would help her to feel differently?" Thus the worker is already in the preliminary stage of task formulation as the client fully examines the target problem.

When it is clear that further discussion will add little to an understanding of the target problem, the worker briefly summarizes the significant features of the problem that must be taken into account.

> **Worker:** You've pointed out a number of important parts of this problem. You've noted that there are no day care centers in your part of town, that the children get upset when they are not in their bed at night, and that you've done a number of favors for your neighbor who lives next door. Now we need to think about what you and I can do to get your day care problem worked out.

Next, formulate the task. Reid and Epstein suggest a number of guidelines for formulating the client's task. "Normally the task evolves from the client's own problem-solving efforts and intentions. The caseworker's function is to help the client shape the best possible course of action to remedy his difficulty" (1972: 106). The task should fit the client's motivation, be feasible, and be desirable.

For the task to fit with the client's motive, it must follow the direction and the force of the client's own push for change. The task probably matches up with what the client *wants* to do about the problem but is afraid to do, has mixed emotions about, or simply doesn't know how to go about doing. Such a task readily reflects the client's thinking, her culture, and the possibilities within her situation. For instance, in the illustration above, the client considers it appropriate for neighbors to help each other out. She really *wants* her neighbor's help but considers it the duty of the neighbor to offer. She doesn't know how to ask for help without feeling upset. Let's suppose she is willing to agree to a task requiring her to find out if the neighbor would be able to help. Successful completion of the task would greatly improve her coping skills. Instead of waiting for someone to offer help, she would learn how to take the initiative and reach out for help. Indeed, if she learns that skill she will be less likely to need the caseworker's assistance in the future with similar problems—those whose resolutions primarily require social skills.

The task should be feasible. Can the task be done by the client? Obviously it's senseless to get the client to agree to a course of action that has a high probability of failure. Actually, we should attempt just the opposite. Develop a task or subtask (a part of or step in a task) that the client will have a 90 percent chance of success in doing. Success early in the problem-solving process greatly encourages the client and adds energy to her effort. Since we know from the beginning that the overall completion of a task, which accomplishes either resolution of the problem or strong movement in that direction is going to be difficult for the client, the worker's responsibility is to design with the client each task in small, achievable parts, and to offer appropriate assistance, such that the client will be successful and learn from doing.

The task should be desirable. Should the task be done? This is an ethical question. Rarely does any course of action lead to altogether positive outcomes for both the client and those with whom she is closely connected. Unfortunately, some things that have to get done have bad as well as good consequences on the individual or those close to her. The mother of two preschool-aged children has chosen to divorce her husband (their father). She has no marketable skills. The husband, though an unsatis-factory mate, is a good breadwinner. He is likely to continue child support long after the divorce is slim. In addition, the children are very attached to him in spite of the fact that he is not a very responsive father. The question must be raised with this client regarding the losses and the gains of solving her marital problem by taking steps to dissolve the marriage.

An elderly client has lived all her life in a four-room frame house which is now impossible to heat and falling apart around her. A low interest housing improvement loan available to the elderly would restore her house but would also require a monthly loan payment whereas she now has no housing costs beyond utilities. On the other hand, she could sell her property and move into a high-rise apartment complex for the elderly and have improved shelter without increasing her financial bur-den. But she would leave her friends and familiar surroundings. How do the losses and gains balance?

Sometimes what the client wants is not good for her immedi-ate family, the community at large, or ultimately even for herself. Shaping the client's task involves carefully assessing the desirability of the proposed actions. This responsibility rests squarely on the shoulders of the caseworker, who may need to challenge the client's ideas and point out probable negative consequences. Where serious danger seems inevitable and the client is adamantly committed to the dangerous course of action, the caseworker must be willing to express clear dis-approval and use her influence as a trusted ally to persuade the client against the intended actions. Such a course of action requires a weighty decision of the worker. Overt disapproval of a client's ideas or actions should be expressed by the caseworker only after all else fails. (Considering consequences and other alternatives is certainly preferable to outright disapproval.)

The final formulation of the task should be brief—one or two sentences—and in the client's words. The task for the elderly lady regarding moving or remodeling might be: "I'll talk to some of the residents in the high-rise apartment and see what they think I should do." In so doing, the client will not only get opinions which may be either positive or negative but also make contacts that may develop into relationships should she decide to move. This task would not completely resolve the problem but would be a step in that direction. It would need to be followed with additional tasks.

The client who wanted the divorce may decide she needs first to make efforts toward improving her marriage. Her task might be: "I'm going to try to get my husband more interested in me as a wife." That task is so broad that the worker will need to help the client shape subtasks which move toward the larger task. Possibilities would include: "I'm going to talk nice to him when he comes home every day. I'm going to do something I usually wouldn't do for him every day." The client probably has other ideas, as well.

Rehearsal. Actions that resolve problems are difficult for the client to perform; otherwise the client would have already resolved the problem. The elderly lady would have made the decision about the move were it not that she has ambivalent feelings as well as inadequate information. For her to talk to residents of the high rise means reaching out, something she hasn't done for a long time. So you ask her, "How will you go about talking to them?" Other similar questions will assist the client in developing a plan—an outline to follow. She responds, "I could call the apartment office and ask to talk to a resident." The caseworker pursues this possibility.

> **Worker:** Let's run through that right now, just like you'd do it. I'll answer the phone as the apartment manager.
>
> **Client:** You mean right now? Me play like I'm calling? (The caseworker nods affirmatively.) O.K. I don't even know the number. (The caseworker offers her telephone book and a pencil and paper.) I've got the number. I'm dialing it.
>
> **Worker:** Hello, Wesley Towers. Mrs. Andrews speaking.

The client hesitates, looks uncertain, and after a brief silence says, "I don't know what to say." The caseworker says, "That's O.K., what do you need to ask the manager?" The process continues until the client is able to carry out the telephone call rehearsal to her satisfaction. Sometimes it helps if the caseworker models for the client how the actions can be carried out. The client then takes the role of the apartment manager and asks the questions that she thinks the apartment manager might ask, followed by the client's taking her own role and the caseworker's being the apartment manager. Although this may seem overly simple, such rehearsals help the client anticipate how to carry out the task as well as give the client practice in doing it. This is basic skill building which can serve this client well in managing other problems. Almost any task can be rehearsed in some way in the interview session.

The balance of the process: task modification, follow-up, and caseworker assignment. Task-focused problem solving is a joint venture of the caseworker and the client in the truest sense of the word. The problem is to be solved by the two working together. Not only does the caseworker engage the client during the interview in both supporting and challenging ways, but she also accepts responsibilities regarding actions on behalf of the client. Contacts with persons in other agencies, visits to the client's home, contacts with family members and employers, worker initiated follow-up contacts with the client: All suggest a very active role for the worker. The client must have a continuing sense that she is carrying the major responsibility for resolving her problem, but that *she is not carrying it alone.* Frequently the agreed on contacts will have been completed before the problem is entirely resolved. The client may feel a need to maintain the contact to the very end.

Most of the time, this alteration in the contract should not be made. Instead, an understanding to touch base in four to six weeks will assure the client of the worker's continuing concern and will demonstrate belief in the client's ability to work out the balance of the problem. The understanding of who initiates the follow-up contact can be left open; but the caseworker is committed to fulfill the agreement no later than the sixth week if the client has not. In public welfare casework, the period may vary, particularly with clients who are permanent service clients. Quarterly contact to review the client's needs can include follow-up on problems previously worked on. Where the problem has been particularly risky for the client a four-to-six-week interim is far more appropriate, however.

*Using the task-focused approach with long-term clients.*Some service clients fit easily into the brief model where termination is anticipated from the first interview of the problem episode. These clients may have had problems requiring assistance in the past; they will likely have problems requiring assistance in the future. Each will be treated as a separate problem with a beginning and a termination of the service relationship. There are also a great many clients who must be carried by a worker for a very long period, months and even years. Many elderly clients fit this description, as do many protective service cases and disability cases. The task-focused model must be slightly modified where extended services are required.

The overall contract with the client should include an understanding that a regularly scheduled interview would occur, perhaps monthly or even quarterly depending on the probability of change occurring in the client's circumstances. More frequent meetings could be arranged at any time at the request of the client. On those occasions when the client requests a contact due to a problem or change in circumstances, the process as outlined (beginning with problem exploration and continuing through follow-up) is used. Having concluded the problem episode the monthly or quarterly contacts are resumed.

The monthly or quarterly contacts focus on the client's current situation and any changes in circumstances. These interviews are *problem searches.* As with all long-term clients, the worker has a good awareness of the probable problem areas. These are explored while, at the same time, the worker is tuned in to any changes she can identify in the client's health, attitudes, life circumstances, or emotions. These changes are clues that should be pursued. For instance, many persons in oppressive situations from which they have little hope of escaping have a pretty negative view of life. They frequently appear to the untrained eye as being depressed. The caseworker knows this sort of client is not likely to be an optimistic, jovial person. But the client appears to have lost a great deal of weight, complains of problems in sleeping and appetite or gastro-intestinal irregularity, these changes indicate that this typically downcast client is now *seriously depressed.* Something out of the ordinary is bothering her, and the caseworker needs to explore for a target problem. Serious consideration must be given as well to making the symptoms of depression the target, probably requiring getting the client medical attention.

Many times these regularly scheduled meetings will turn up no problem, however, and will simply serve to maintain a supportive relationship between worker and client. It is very important for the client to know that the contacts will continue even if no problem is identified. You wouldn't want the client to manufacture a problem to retain the relationship. Regularly scheduled meetings do not foster dependence; rather, they maintain for the high-risk client a viable problem-solving mechanism where otherwise none would exist.

Protective service cases: special consideration. The extended nature of the protective service client relationship is likely a reflection of the agency's legally mandated responsibility, not the client's expressed need or desire. Although the caseworker will make every effort to develop a positive relationship that will be productive for the client (the parent as well as the child), the primary reason the service relationship exists is to protect the child against further abuse or neglect. This, of course, has to be made clear at the outset. It also needs to be made clear that the state considers the removal of the risk to the child the responsibility of the parent and the caseworker. The caseworker sets up a contract which includes periodic problem searches as outlined above and implementation of a plan protecting the child until the parent, through the problem-solving process, sufficiently modifies the problem circumstances to eliminate the risk to the child. This is a two-pronged approach which is obviously connected but which must be treated separately if the client is to be effectively engaged.

In all cases where the client is involuntarily involved, the caseworker has two problems. The unsatisfied wants of the client must be identified and addressed, and at the same time, the mandated problems of the referring agency must be attended to. If the client is unwilling to name an unsatisfied want, the caseworker may find the client more receptive if deficiencies in the client's resources are given early attention. Having identified deficits in food, shelter, clothing, or medical care, caseworker and client tasks should immediately be outlined so that the client's concrete needs will be supplied. Such actions usually impress the client with the caseworker's motive to help and tends to move the client toward full partnership in the effort. This is particularly important with impoverished adults who themselves were probably neglected and abused children. They need to see the caseworker as a caring person first of all.

As the client becomes more involved in identifying target problems, formulating and carrying out actions to resolve these problems, the caseworker can reward the forward movement of the client by modifying the imposed protective service plan. The principle of positive reinforcement is applied again as the worker identifies the specific actions of the client which have merited the change by the worker. The worker can further interpret this positive reinforcement as a natural consequence of good parenting, noting that the client will no doubt identify other natural rewards for good parenting, such as increased responsiveness of her children and increased respect from her neighbors. Eventually, the protective service episode can be converted into an extended, periodic, problem-solving contact which will be terminated by plan.

Some clients refer themselves or are referred and can identify no target problem. Occasionally a person will request assistance from a caseworker and yet be unable to identify a problem on which he or she is willing to work. This person may have lots of generalized complaints and be truly miserable, yet the willingness to act on the problem is lacking. This unwillingness can be related to the client's hesitancy in speaking openly in the first meeting with a stranger. It can be related to the client's shame, embarrassment, or fear growing out of the problem circumstance. Here it is not just the newness of the worker-client relationship which creates the difficulty. More than that, it is the distress the client experiences in recounting the problem to another person. Getting it out in the open means more directly facing the problem and the pain involved. As long as the client doesn't talk about the problem, she is able to some degree to hide it from herself. She hides it in her head.

When confronted by this situation, the worker, as the first interview in this problem episode is about to end, makes clear to the client that she apparently is troubled by a number of things. These are listed by the worker in the order of significance identified by the client. She asks again if the client is willing to focus on one out of the list as a place to begin resolving the trouble. If the client continues to express uncertainty, the worker suggests that the client may wish to return home and think for the next few days about their discussion. The worker offers a specific time for a second interview to continue the problem search, noting to the client an expectation that the two of them will be able to find something to work on that will make a significant difference in the client's situation. The worker notes with warmth and concern that the next session will have to identify a target problem, since only two interviews can be used to identify the problem that the client is willing to work on. In this way, the caseworker is using the limits of time to push the client to work. The worker is attempting to create a sense of urgency for the client about resolving her problem. The client may be told, as well, that if she decides on the problem before the agreed-upon meeting time, she may call the worker and set an earlier appointment. The worker thus makes obvious her availability and immediate concern with the client's distress while making it clear to the client that the two cannot proceed without the client's decision.

What if the client makes no decision at the conclusion of the second interview? During the course of the second interview, the worker listens carefully for differences in the way the client presents her circumstances from the first interview. These are noted to the client. The worker identifies for the client the levels of intensity of emotion associated with various topics discussed, responding empathically to the emotion and attempting to move the client toward a deeper sense of her involvement. The worker carefully notes what the client brings up first in the interview, and any repetitions which occur in topics or references to people. These are identified for the client with a question such as "This seems to be at the heart of your problem; is it?" or "Does this mean that this is what we need to work on?" Notice that the phrasing of these questions puts the client in a position of making a decision rather than exploring further the dilemma. Such questions, which can be answered with a "yes" or "no" or other one or two-word answers, are called "closed questions," as opposed to the open questions which generate exploration. Closed questions, when carefully phrased with material drawn from the client's presentation, are very effective in helping the client make a decision.

If, at the close of the second interview, the client is still unable or unwilling to identify a focus to work on, the worker summarizes their effort of two interviews and states with warmth and concern that she will be unable to set another appointment without a target problem to work on. At this point the worker suggests a new alternative. She suggests they try working on one of the problems the client has stated as a "temporary target problem." Example:

> **Caseworker**: I've been listening to you, and I believe you've got a lot to gain by doing something about your housing situation. Would you be willing to try that as your target problem for two weeks?

The uncertain client may welcome this as a reasonable suggestion and agree. On the other hand, the client may continue, unwilling to focus on any problem. If this happens, the client is

offered another interview in three months to do another problem search.

An agreement is made about who will make the call to set up
the appointment. Many caseworkers prefer to leave this responsibility with the client with the understanding that the worker
will call if she doesn't hear from the client in the appointed
month. The client may refuse this offer. Whether she does or
does not, the caseworker makes clear as she concludes the
interview that she will at any time welcome a telephone call
indicating that the client has identified the problem focus to be
addressed. In that event, an appointment would be set immediately to continue identifying the appropriate task or tasks for
the client to do and the required related actions to be taken by
the worker.

Evaluation: Have you helped the client? The task-focused
approach to problem solving eliminates the guesswork in evaluating whether the client has been helped or not. Since the task
which the client undertakes is a major step toward problem
resolution, the completion of that task or demonstration of the
task is the sign that the client has been helped. It is not enough
that the client says she feels better; that may just be the result
of talking to the worker and, unless talking to the worker was
one of the client's tasks, is not a real problem resolution. The
task must be completed or demonstrated to the client and the
caseworker's satisfaction to meet the standard for successful
casework set up in the contract which the two established after
the target was identified and committed to.

Some difficulties in completing the task are anticipated, since
the client *is* working on something she has not been able to
resolve prior to the casework relationship. As noted previously,
she may wish to give up the task. A part of ongoing evaluation
must focus on the need to modify the task and in some
circumstances to eliminate the task and to substitute a new one.
Before such a radical change is made, however, careful consideration must be given by both the caseworker and the client to
the need for change. A task change in some circumstances may
spare the client the strain of working on the problem but

further convince her that the problem is beyond her capacity to resolve. Encouragement, rehearsal, and breaking the task down into subtasks accompanied by appropriate supportive actions on behalf of the client by the worker should be carefully pursued as a result of the ongoing evaluation.

Some clients are not helped. For some of us, it is unacceptable for a client not to resolve her problem as a result of our joint efforts. This suggests an unwillingness to face a fact of life. Casework is not always successful. The best efforts by both client and caseworker may result in no progress. Has the client been helped? We must answer, "Not enough!" Was it the worker's fault or the client's? The worker and her supervisor will no doubt seek some answers to that question. They may find none. What was done in casework simply didn't accomplish the desired end. For the most part this is apparent because the client has not completed or made an adequate demonstration of the task. Thus, there is no visible change in the target problem. The client may terminate the process of attempting the task, or she may simply decide the problem is not important enough to command so much of her attention and so withdraw from the casework agreement. Her circumstances may change and other matters require immediate attention. These factors are not brought to the caseworker's attention because the client either leaves the geographic area or perceives the problem as not appropriate to the caseworker's responsibility. The caseworker must be careful that she does not accept the blame for failure to meet the casework contract unless there is clear and specific reason to believe she made an error. A worker who considers herself responsible for a failure should discuss the situation with her supervisor in order to get another point of view and to learn how to correct mistakes if they have indeed been made.

Exercises

Think about one of your clients. What problem might she have identified as being the one of greatest importance to her? Explore that problem in your mind. Write below: How does your client describe the problem, how does the client see herself fitting into the problem, how does she see herself affected, what does she believe about other persons' involvement in the problem? What else do you know about her and her problem situation?

_____

_____

_____

_____

Remembering that a task appropriate for the client to attempt in resolving the above problem must be culturally appropriate and sufficiently difficult that the client would not attempt it outside of the casework relationship, construct a task that you think your client might suggest or consider.

_____

_____

_____

_____

6

PROBLEMS IN LIVING

Problems in living, like the people who have them, come in many shapes and sizes. Some are like a bad cold: They linger on and on seemingly must be endured until they go away, since nothing we do seems to help much. Others come upon us like a storm, shaking us to the roots and demanding to be dealt with. All problems in living that are appropriately worked with in social casework have at least one thing in common. Whether a lingering problem or a crisis, each represents an unfulfilled want of an individual or individuals. Reid defines a "want" as the experience of a person who has identified something desirable and has an accompanying tension resulting from not having it (1978: 47).

When a person expresses a problem as a want, he may state either the circumstances which caused the problem or the solution the person considers needed. In the first instance, the person might say, "I want to stop arguing with my children!" An example of the second is the person who says, "I want to get new shoes for my children!" In each situation, there is a clear need specified by the person with an accompanying set of emotions reflecting distress—usually anger, anxiety, frustration or depression, or a mixture of these. Each such problem can be effectively approached with the task-focused model just presented. In fact, getting a client to talk of what he wants or needs, essentially discussing the goal of the casework, can be a very useful way of identifying the target problem.

Some people live in such difficult circumstances that an outsider finds it hard to understand precisely when the circumstances do or do not add up to a problem. Only the person in the situation can say. Sometimes the person's circumstances appear the same as they have been for months or years, yet all of a sudden the person wants things to be different. At another time, the circumstances appear to be similar, yet the person expresses no desire for things to be different. By our definition, only when the person wants things different is there a problem to work on. Each of us has experienced changes in our willingness to accept things as they are. At one point we may be willing to live with our situation; at another time we may be sufficiently upset to attempt to bring about change and another time be apathetic and not care. *This* problem-solving approach assumes that a person must be engaged in problem-solving *while she wants change* if there is to be a high probability of change occurring.

Reid (1978) suggests a number of problem types. Among those a typical caseworker may have clients identify are: (1) interpersonal conflict; (2) difficulties in role performance; (3) reactive emotional distress; (4) inadequate resources; (5) problems with formal organizations; and (6) decision problems. Some clients have difficulties in all of these areas at a given moment. They must be helped to decide what they most need to work on.

Let's consider each problem type in detail and some possible tasks the client might do as a move toward resolution. Our purpose in dividing the various problems in living into problem types is to identify the most effective way each problem type can be handled in the task-focused approach. In the discussion of each problem type specific guidelines are noted for caseworker intervention.

Interpersonal conflict. Two people who are involved directly and intensely in verbal or physical abuse or who have such differences of opinion that their discussions regarding certain topics are in fact bitter arguments are considered to be having an interpersonal conflict. Mild or occasional differences of opinion, arguments, or verbal fights should be viewed by the workers as communication problems between people which require no casework intervention. At most, such problems of moderate conflict should be approached as a difficulty in role performance or an excessive emotional reaction to conflict on the part of the client. (Each of these problem types will be discussed later in this section.)

Interpersonal conflicts occur most frequently in families. But situations that fall into this category do arise between neighbors, in the work setting, and with persons in formal organizations with whom one deals regularly and intimately. Interpersonal conflicts cannot be resolved without *both* persons' agreeing that a problem exists, and *both* persons' expressing willingness to work on the problem together. It is altogether unrealistic for an interpersonal conflict to be selected as a target problem unless both parties can be in contact with the worker. Where only one of the persons in the conflict is involved with the caseworker, the client should be led to understand the appropriate target problem is the client's emotional reaction to the conflict or deficits in role performance. Tasks can be arranged with the client to assure a change in one of those areas even though the conflict will likely continue. Of course, the interpersonal conflict will cease if the client discontinues any further contact with the person. Here are a few problem statements with accompanying tasks that illustrate interpersonal conflict as a target problem:

Case Illustration: Mrs. J lives alone with her thirteen-year-old son, Joe. For the past year Mrs. J has reported to the caseworker increasing difficulties in getting along with Joe. She is deeply concerned about his choice of friends, his staying away from home after dark, and, most recently, his unwillingness to attend school. Her greatest concern, however, is the verbal and near-physical fighting that occurs with him nearly every day. Joe is almost as big as she is and she worries that if the conflict doesn't stop soon he will begin to abuse her physically as his father did. As she describes these arguments she expresses a mixture of anger, fear, and anxiety in varying degrees of intensity. Since Mrs. J's greatest want is to "stop having these run-ins with Joe" rather than to get him to go to school or to behave differently, her problem is considered to be one of interpersonal conflict. The problem statement might be:

Problem Statement for Target Problem: Mrs. J and her thirteen-year-old son, Joe, have verbal fights every day over his behavior.

The worker explains to Mrs. J the necessity of involving Joe in the casework if the conflict between the two is to be lessened or resolved. On the basis of this explanation, the task defined below is agreed upon as the necessary first toward Mrs. J's goal.

Goal: Reduction of conflict between Mrs. J and Joe, her son.

Task: Mrs. J agrees to try to have Joe with her for her next interview.

Since this is a problem in interpersonal conflict between two persons, both must be involved in deciding what, if anything, is to be done. The client's first task, then, is to get Joe to meet with her and the caseworker. This will not be easy. If Joe is doing pretty much as he pleases, he is not likely to be thrilled about meeting with the caseworker and his mother. Mrs. J will probably be a bit anxious, even fearful, at the prospect of getting Joe to the next interview.

The caseworker must use the balance of the interview to explore in depth Mrs. J's ideas and feelings as she approaches the task. Having gotten the feelings out in the open, the caseworker must lead her into a rehearsal of how she intends to go about bringing Joe to the next interview. This will no doubt involve an explanation to Joe about his required attendance in the interview. Playing the part of Joe, the worker will interact with Mrs. J as she shows how she will go about talking to Joe.

Since Mrs. J usually has conflicts with Joe, it is important that her approach and explanation to him about the interview not end in an argument or verbal fight. As Mrs. J interacts with the caseworker in the rehearsal, the worker first responds cooperatively, agreeing, as Joe, to attend the interview. Mrs. J is asked if Joe would have responded similarly. Mrs. J will no doubt respond, "No!" Mrs. J is then asked to play the part of Joe, behaving as she thinks he would behave, while the caseworker takes Mrs. J's part. *This is a crucial point.* The worker has the opportunity to model for the client a way of approaching and explaining to Joe the necessity of his attending the next interview.

First the worker must demonstrate a *nonaccusing* attitude. She will do this by *avoiding the use of "you"* as the subject of a sentence in her conversation. She will use "I" and "we" instead. She might say, "Joe, I'm tired of the way we get into an argument about something every day. I want to stop arguing with you." Joe, at this point, if he has been listening, will be surprised that he has not been accused of anything. The worker can continue as Mrs. J. "I told Mrs. Harris at the welfare office about our arguments, and she said she could help us stop arguing. Do you want her to help get me off your back?" Mrs. J (acting the part of Joe) is going to find it hard to continue her negative reaction to the worker (as Mrs. J) but will probably make an attempt. The worker (as Mrs. J) might respond, "I hope you'll want to see an end to our problems because I'm determined that the arguing is going to stop. I told Mrs. Harris we would both go to her office next week on Tuesday after school so she could help us stop arguing." After this rehearsal, the worker asks Mrs. J to comment on how the worker played Mrs. J's part. What did she notice about the way the worker played her part? Mrs. J may note that she did not get the *feeling* of being accused. The worker may have to explain how she structured her statements in order to be nonaccusing. Now she will ask Mrs. J to be herself and try approaching Joe (played by the worker) as a nonaccusing parent.

Again, the worker is careful not to overwhelm Mrs. J in the role play. As Mrs. J proceeds, the rehearsal may have to stop for some coaching and encouragement. The worker is careful *not* to give Mrs. J specific instructions, since Mrs. J's action must fit with her personality and culture. But the worker does offer comments and suggestions regarding the way the client carries out the task. After Mrs. J has got through a rehearsal fairly successfully, the worker will suggest one more rehearsal "to meet the test of Joe's being hard to deal with." At this point the worker acts more negatively in playing Joe, although again being careful not to defeat Mrs. J. The goal of the rehearsal period is for Mrs. J to try out ways she and the worker consider will more likely succeed than fail in performing her task. She should leave the interview with an attitude of optimism toward accomplishing a difficult task.

Let us now suppose Mrs. J returns for the next interview with Joe. The worker must use all the helping skills earlier cited to engage Joe. Joe must feel safe and welcome. Joe must agree that the constant conflict between mother and son is a problem for him also. He, too, must want to do something about it. If he agrees to the statement of the target problem as it was formulated by his mother and the caseworker, then the worker engages the two in formulating tasks which mother and son will carry out in reducing their conflict. These tasks should emerge from a discussion by all parties. The worker must be careful to keep the discussion balanced; mother and son each should talk about the same amount of time. An appropriate set of tasks usually takes the form of a *quid pro quo*—a trade off—an "I'll do this if you do that" arrangement around specific problems. For instance:

Mother's task: I will stop fussing when Joe is no more than an hour after dark arriving home as long as Joe goes to school each day. I'll stay off his back about friends.

Joe's task: I'll go to school each day and get home within an hour after dark as long as she stays off my back. If I don't go to school or am later than an hour after dark, I'll listen to her fussing without getting angry.

Both of these tasks will be difficult for Mrs. J and for Joe to perform. The caseworker outlines her own task to both Joe and his mother as that of letting each know how well they are accomplishing their tasks. This is a difficult role for the worker. Both Joe and his mother will be watching to see if the worker is fair and objective. The worker must be willing to say to each in a nonaccusing fashion, "It sounds like you may have messed up that time. What do you think?" Each interview after the tasks have been formulated is spent in evaluating how well the agreement has been carried out the previous week. Additional tasks may be formulated, or ongoing tasks may be modified if both mother and son are in agreement. Six to eight contacts should be agreed on at the time the tasks are formulated. These contacts should extend over a three to four-month period, with the last two- to three contacts occurring a month apart. The first two contacts may need to be within a few days of one another, followed by weekly, then monthly interviews.

Rehearsals during these interviews are closer to "trial runs." Since both Joe and his mother are present, their responses are not role plays as much as they are genuine encounters. These trial runs are handled similarly to the rehearsals described above, except that one person is always acting the part of an observer who comments on the behavior of the other two. The worker should avoid analyzing the behavior of Joe and his mother. Instead, the worker focuses her effort on getting both Joe and Mrs. J to act out their observations as the trial run or rehearsal continues. It sometimes helps for the parent and child to reverse roles in the rehearsal or for the caseworker to play either the child or parent role to model the desired behavior.

Interpersonal conflicts are not resolved easily. Each of us knows that such situations have to be worked at over long periods. The worker's involvement is limited but has the very important effect of getting two people who are at a dead end to work together, thus restoring a new balance to their situation. If the clients have learned enough in the process, they may be able to carry on alone, or they may come back for another sequence at a later time. In either event, new coping mechanisms that reduce interpersonal conflict will have been established. Workers who view this case description as a bit scary should take heart. Although it is the most difficult of the problem types with which you will deal, it is also the most rewarding in which to see favorable results.

Interpersonal conflicts are among the most difficult to resolve through casework or any other approach. It is possible, though not highly probable, that Mrs. J will not be able to bring her thirteen-year-old to the next interview. If she arrives without Joe, the worker can spend the interview in refining and rehearsing how Mrs. J can carry out the task of bringing Joe to the next interview (if Mrs. J wants to continue that effort), or the problem may be redefined as Mrs. J's difficulty in role performance or her over-reaction to conflict, two other types of problems—but types which require only Mrs. J's involvement for resolution. We'll carry the case study of Mrs. J forward as we look at this situation as a difficulty in role performance.

Difficulties in role performance. If Joe will not participate in the interviews, Mrs. J may have to redefine her problem as a difficulty in performing a social role; in this instance, the role of mother. He want must turn from a reduction in conflict with her son to a new look at herself and how well she is meeting her own expectations as a parent. She will also need to consider how well she is meeting Joe's expectations of her as his mother. Finally, she must note the differences that exist between what she expects of herself in performing the role of mother and what Joe expects of her in that role. Another aspect of role performance is what the community expects of the person performing a given role.

Look again at Mrs. J. She expects of herself as mother to tell her son what is required of him. He is to go to school, come home at dark, and have appropriate friends. When he does not do these things, she considers it a mother's place to scold him. It is not clear what other expectations she has of herself as a mother. These would have to be explored with her. Neither is it clear how much responsibility she considers hers in seeing that

Joe goes to school, comes in at dark, and keeps appropriate company ("responsibility" here as opposed merely to telling him he should do these things). Joe's expectations of his mother are not very clear, though we may assume he doesn't expect his mother to do very much to make him go to school, come in at dark, or keep good friends. His expectations are based on what she has done to date, which appears to be only shouting and making occasional threats. The expectations of the community regarding appropriate mothering of a thirteen-year-old boy may vary, but state law expects her to see that he is in school and at home at night—and, to a certain extent, expects her to see that his friends are not delinquents.

> **Mrs. J's problem statement could be:** Mrs. J. does not exercise adequate control over Joe.
> **Her goal then might be:** Mrs. J. wants to be more effective in setting limits for Joe.
> **An appropriate task** for Mrs. J. would be for her to be sure that Joe gets to school every day.

Performance of this task would require Mrs. J's taking steps to see that Joe arrived at school each day and to know if he stayed throughout the day. She would also have to decide what she would do if he did not arrive at school and if he left school during the day. These intended actions would be discussed with the worker and then rehearsed. She would also decide what she would do if Joe did as asked. The principle of positive reinforcement mentioned earlier is one which Mrs. J obviously needs to learn. She needs to decide how she will make it more worthwhile for Joe to go to school than to stay away. All of this can be discussed with the caseworker, focusing on how Mrs. J can say she is pleased with Joe's going to school as well as what she can do that will encourage Joe (perhaps fixing something to eat he especially likes). The role performances requiring verbal behavior should be rehearsed with the caseworker.

Although we have considered only the role of mother, social roles include any family or community role that we take on or earn--such as employee, student, client, and the like. Difficulties in role performance may come about as a result of: (1) *inadequate skills* to meet the expectations of oneself, others, or the community regarding how to perform the role; (2) *conflicts* between one's own expectations about how to perform the role and how, others or the community expect the role to be performed; (3) *having to perform two different roles* at the same time (such as being an employee and being a mother). Mrs. J's problems seem to be focused in the area of inadequate skills to perform her role. With patience and encouragement from the caseworker these can be learned. It may be true also that in learning new skills and applying them with Joe, she may be less inclined to involve herself in arguing or verbal fighting with him, thus gaining some relief in her first priority target problem, that of interpersonal conflict.

Reactive emotional distress. Had Mrs. J defined her problem as her own emotional reaction to having conflict with her son, rather than the conflict itself, her case would have been one of reactive emotional distress, in which case she would want help with her feelings rather than with the cause of the feelings. Her reason—or need (for it may not be reasonable)—for wanting help with her feelings, rather than with the situation that may be giving rise to her feelings, may be that she is so upset that she can't get herself together enough to deal with the situation. Or she may consider the situation so out of her control that nothing she can do will resolve it. In the case of Mrs. J, we certainly would consider this as starting where she is; but, out of concern for Joe, we would certainly expect to move next to a target problem directly involving the situation with Joe. To illustrate this problem focus more satisfactorily, let's take a different situation.

Case illustration: Mr. D is a disability client. During his late teens he was injured in a work-related accident that left him crippled in both legs and with a spine injury which causes constant pain. Mr. D lives with his elderly mother. Efforts at vocational rehabilitation have been unsuccessful due to Mr. D's limited mobility and his frequent inability to get out of bed due to pain. At those times, he becomes very depressed about his situation and wants the caseworker to help him to feel better.

Mr. D has identified his target problem as being depressed about his situation of living constantly in pain.

Goal: Mr. D would like to be less upset by his situation.

A possible task: Mr. D might agree to go to his physician and explore a change in his medication or other ways of reducing the pain.

As an alternative, Mr. D might agree to write down how he experiences the pain in his body.

Since this is a problem that the client has identified concerning his emotional reaction to a situation, the focus must be on changing feelings. Talking with the caseworker about those feelings, if the worker is empathic in her responses, will cause the depression to lift somewhat. But the most effective way to deal with depression is to do something about it. Thus, the tasks which are designed with the client involve his actively doing something related to his depression. Talking to the doctor may not bring any new relief from his pain, but it will get the client moving again, with an accompanying reduction in his depression (but not from his pain, which apparently cannot be controlled). It is important in this situation for the caseworker to identify with the client her need to be in touch with the doctor so that she can update the doctor on her casework activities with Mr. D. This is necessary so that the caseworker can explain to the physician that Mr. D is depressed and that she is trying to get him moving to keep him from being further depressed. Without caseworker contact, the doctor might fail to recognize Mr. D's depression and be impatient with his complaint, since Mr. D has been told many times that nothing can be done for his pain. Through the caseworker's careful intervention, the physician can be alerted to the need for understanding, and perhaps a

substitution of a medication can be tried or some other varia-
tion of treatment offered to give Mr. D some positive reinforcement for doing something about his depression. Both the physician and the caseworker can stay alert in their common effort
to use every means possible to help Mr. D avoid becoming an
abuser of alcohol or drugs. This can best be done by keeping
him actively working on handling his pain through other means.

Four to six interviews will probably be necessary to accomplish the task outlined. No more than one interview will be
necessary to identify the target problem in a situation such as
this. A second interview may be necessary for exploration of
the problem in depth and formulating the task for Mr. D to
accomplish. This may require a number of subtasks to deal with
transportation, the appointment with the physician, and so
forth. Since depression can be a debilitating condition, the more
specific small tasks that can be readily handled in a brief fashion
the more likely Mr. D will be to accomplish the task and move
toward more normal functioning. The balance of the interviews
is spent in reviewing efforts at accomplishing the task, rehearsing interpersonal behavior required in task accomplishment,
reformulating tasks, and the caseworker's reporting on any
activities she has engaged in on behalf of the client. If Mr. D
formulates a task such as writing about his pain, some of the
interview time would be spent in reviewing what he has written.
Attempts to help Mr. D to express his feelings more effectively
through this fashion may culminate in his developing an additional means to cope.

Inadequate resources. The most common problem presented
to a public welfare caseworker is that of inadequate resources.
In such a situation, the client lacks tangible, concrete resources
such as money, housing, food, transportation, employment,
child care, clothing, or medicine. Problems where the client's
access to the resource is being blocked by an agency or organization are considered under a separate category, *Problems with
Formal Organizations.* Problems of inadequate resources are
those where the focus is on the client's lack of resources and

where there is no apparent hindrance outside the client in obtaining the resource. Since the cases above have illustrated relatively simple steps in the problem-solving process, this case (similar to one cited by Reid, 1978: 47) is more realistic in presenting the complex task and the need for not only the client but also the caseworker and other persons to perform specific tasks in order for the problem to be resolved.

> **Case illustration**: Mrs. W, an elderly woman in poor health, is deeply concerned about her granddaughter, a three year old whom she is raising. The child has been recently diagnosed as having developmental problems. Specifically, she is not toilet-trained, has limited speech, gets uncontrollably angry, and physically assaults others without provocation. The whereabouts of the mother and the father are unknown, and Mrs. W has sole responsibility for the child.

> The target problem agreed upon is the child's difficult behavior.

> **Goal**: Mrs. W wants to obtain the necessary help to assist her with her granddaughter.

The following tasks were identified and agreed upon for the client, the worker, and others.

Worker tasks:

(1) Arrange for child care specialists to make home visits and train Mrs. W in how to toilet train the child.
(2) Arrange for part-day attendance of the child at a center for developmentally disabled children.
(3) Transport and accompany Mrs. W and the child to the evaluation center for periodic visits.
(4) Provide Mrs. W with a monthly schedule of professional appointments and activities for the child.

Client tasks:

(1) Get the child ready for her appointments.

(2) Get the child to speech therapy weekly.

(3) Learn from the child care specialists ways of toilet training and managing the child's disruptive behavior.

Tasks for others:

(1) Mrs. Thomas, child care specialist, will visit Mrs. W at home and provide the necessary training for her in managing the child.

(2) Mrs. Jones, public health nurse at the Evaluation Center, will monitor the child's medical condition and see that proper medication is available.

(3) Mrs. Arnold, director of the child care center, will provide monthly reports to Mrs. W and the caseworker on the child's progress.

This case clearly illustrates the need for cooperation and coordination between professionals in resolving a client's needs when a problem of inadequate resources is the target problem. The caseworker is the coordinator and facilitator of communication between all parties. This is not simply paper work but involves the use of her relationship in her contacts with Mrs. W and the others who are significantly involved in the case. Interacting in a warm, respectful, and empathic manner with all parties will enable the worker to be tuned in on how well things are going. She can identify the need for task adjustment or additional tasks as the case progresses. Being "on top of the case" in this manner guarantees that progressive movement toward problem resolution is assured. In such situations the worker may keep limited contact for a period of months through accompanying Mrs. W and the child to the Evaluation Center on their periodic visits and through regular telephone contacts with others involved. Follow-up and monitoring by the caseworker can terminate when, in her judgment, Mrs. W has solid contacts with the service providers in the other agencies and so needs no further assistance from the worker. This is not an open-ended arrangement, although it may be extended over three to four months. Even this extended time frame can be specified to all persons involved as the tasks are formulated. But where many persons depend on one another, the plan frequently needs adjustment, and *flexibility* is the rule of thumb in maintaining interagency cooperation and coordination.

Problems with formal organizations. This particular category is for situations where the client is attempting to get a needed service from and agency and is blocked in that effort by someone in that agency. In large agencies, this can happen when a client is referred from one worker to another for a particular service and cannot obtain it. Sometimes the problem is one of eligibility. Most federal programs are governed by complex regulations. Those regulations change frequently. As a result, clients may find themselves attempting to obtain a needed service and being denied access to that service by a staff member who thinks the client is ineligible. Many times the determination of eligibility is a matter not of hard facts but of the judgment of a staff member—whose judgment may be in error. Denial of access to services to an eligible client may result as well through agency policies regarding appropriate referral procedures and waiting lists. Most clients simply are unable to cut through the red tape that can be generated by an agency. Occasionally there is a problem of communication. The client goes to the correct agency and is clearly eligible but is unable to state her problem in such a way that the agency staff person agrees that the service is appropriate to the client's need. In each of these instances the client needs a professional to assist her in gaining access to the services provided by the agency. The public welfare caseworker frequently finds herself in this position. Her role is that of client advocate and facilitator in getting the services needed.

Case illustration: Let's suppose that Mrs. W, who is mentioned in the case illustration above, wasn't able to get the needed evaluation of her granddaughter, Cindy. She comes to the public welfare office and tells her caseworker the details about Cindy's problems and states that a neighbor had recommended she go to the evaluation center for the developmentally disabled for help. She explains that she called the center and was told there is a waiting list and that she would need to be referred by a physician or another appropriate professional. Mrs. W explains further that she has no physician, since none will take Medicaid. She doesn't know what to do.

Mrs. W has attempted to use the services of the appropriate agency. She did not get beyond the person who answered the telephone, probably a clerical person not trained to make judgments about the severity of problems and the need to make exceptions to agency policy. If Mrs. W is to get the needed services, her caseworker must assist her. As a result of their discussion in their first interview, it is easy for the caseworker and the client to come to a clear statement of the target problem.

The target problem agreed upon is that Mrs. W is unable to have Cindy evaluated at the Evaluation Center.

Goal: Mrs. W wants Cindy evaluated at the Evaluation Center or another appropriate agency.

The following tasks were agreed upon for both the worker and the client:

Worker tasks:

(1) The worker will call the intake supervisor at the Evaluation Center to discuss referral of Mrs. W and Cindy.
(2) The worker will arrange transportation to the center.

Client task:

(1) Mrs. W will call for an appointment when notified by the worker that the referral has been made.
(2) Mrs. W will take Cindy for her evaluation on the day of the appointment.

The tasks have been arranged in the expectation that the worker will have no difficulty in getting an early appointment for Mrs. W and Cindy based on the information regarding the severity of the problem that she will provide. (The worker has obtained the necessary signed release of information.) It is most important that the worker approach the intake supervisor with this assumption, an assumption based on professional respect. The caseworker begins the interaction, probably over the telephone, stating her need to refer Mrs. W. She is careful not to mention that Mrs. W has unsuccessfully attempted a contact. Her purpose at this point is solely to get Mrs. W and Cindy seen at the earliest possible time, not to improve the Evaluation Center's intake procedure of personnel actions. Respect is conveyed between professionals by courteously and concisely giving the other professional the necessary information for her to make an informed decision. Respect for another professional is always based on the assumption that the other professional is no less interested in your client than you, and equally concerned about getting needed services to those most at risk, children, the elderly, and handicapped persons. Approaching another professional in this matter nearly always generates the same kind of respectful response, so that the caseworker is viewed as a person whose information is accurate and whose judgment as to the critical nature of the situation should merit consideration. Only after the appointment has been made by Mrs. W should the caseworker take up her additional concern with the intake supervisor regarding Mrs. W's unsuccessful attempt at making an appointment. If the referral relationship has been one of respect, then the caseworker's information will more likely be heard as concern than as criticism.

I think the probabilities are very high that the above approach with another professional will result in getting the client's need met. But since the intake supervisor might be cooperative, we need to consider what actions the caseworker should take in that event. As a rule, interagency problems that cannot be handled by direct service staff have to be taken to a higher level of authority in both agencies. The caseworker should organize her information concisely and clearly in writing. In particular, she should be able to document the seriousness of the case. This may mean another interview, perhaps a home visit, where the worker can view firsthand Cindy's behavior. She should note how Mrs. W's health and age limit her and make this a priority case of high risk to both Cindy and Mrs. W. With these facts in hand the caseworker can review the situation with her supervisor, who may feel the agency director needs to make the contact with the director of the evaluation center. We'll hope that the director is successful; but if she is not, the caseworker is back at the position of finding an alternate means of securing an evaluation, perhaps through a private psychologist or psychiatrist or another agency with an evaluation unit. The worker's task is not complete until she has secured adequate professional consultation regarding the special needs of Cindy and Mrs. W.

Decision problems: between a hard place and a rock. That's what it is like to face a particularly difficult decision. When a person presents a problem in making a decision, it is usually because no matter how the person decides, the decision will be costly. Such decisions involve "value dilemmas." These are situations where the person cannot avoid a decision, yet each alternative is like a blurred picture, somehow out of focus. Some of what will be gained through each alternative seems clear, and some of what will be lost seems clear. Things become blurred and unclear when the person is confronted with choosing between or among the alternatives. That's when and where a client will present a problem. Remember that this doesn't mean the person is generally indecisive. It means only that she is hung up on this decision. Let's look again at the elderly lady whose house is deteriorating around her.

Case illustration: Mrs. L is an eighty-year-old widow who has lived alone in her four-room frame house for the past thirty years. She is quite happy in her familiar surroundings, but the house is now falling down around her and is impossible to heat. Last winter Mrs. L was hospitalized once for pneumonia, and the prospects for her health are not good if things remain the same. Mrs. L qualifies for a low-interest housing improvement loan that could restore her house. However, the loan would have to be repaid in monthly installments. Presently her only housing costs are her utilities. Her only income is her Old Age Assistance and SSI. The added monthly payment will require a reduction in money presently being spent on essentials. On the other hand, Mrs. L could sell her property. It happens to be located next to a shopping center and is quite valuable. With the money from the sale she could move into a high-rise apartment complex for the elderly. The income from the sale of the property would easily cover her rent for many years with a good bit to spare. But moving means Mrs. L would leave her familiar surroundings, her friends of many years, and many of the furnishings in her home which she considers too worn to move.

The target problem is Mrs. L's decision on how to improve her housing.

Goal: Mrs. L wants to decide what to do about her housing.

The following tasks are agreed upon by client and worker:

Client tasks:

(1) Talk to friends about how moving would affect their contact with each other.
(2) Talk to some of the residents of the high rise about how moving affected them.
(3) Make a list of the furnishings she could take with her if she moved.

Worker tasks:

(1) Call the local office of the Department of Housing and Urban Development to see if a nonrepayable grant can be arranged for Mrs. L.
(2) Call the Council on Aging to determine if repairs can be arranged through their "fix-it program" if the materials can be obtained through donations from building supply houses.
(3) Call a realtor friend to check on other property Mrs. L might rent near where she currently lives.
(4) Talk to Mr. Friday at the local radio station about finding means to assist Mrs. L in staying in her home.

Multiple tasks are used with the client, since the tasks (with the exception of making a list of furnishings which could be moved) are similar. These are actually subtasks of the larger task which Mrs. L is attempting—to weigh the costs of moving to the high rise. The worker knows that, in performing the tasks of talking to friends and residents, the client will become more aware not only of how much her friends mean to her but also that there are other people just like her in the high rise. She may or may not receive encouragement, but she will have made a beginning toward new relationships should she move. She will also have begun working out how she could maintain contact with her friends should she move.

The worker's tasks are aimed at gathering every possible piece of information which might aid the client. If no way can be arranged to repair Mrs. L's house without cost, her caseworker will have to develop other tasks with Mrs. L, tasks which will enable her to move with little trauma into either the high rise or another rental property. One final word: Great patience is required in working with a person of advanced age around a change in living arrangements. The time frame should be as extended as the weather or health of the person dictates. Otherwise, a crisis of unnecessarily great proportions may be created.

The next section on problems of living concerns those particular problems which usually are crisis events in a person's life. Some decision problems, such as Mrs. L's, must be viewed as potential crises. In fact, if Mrs. L ultimately has to move, her decision will have placed her into a life crisis which she will not be able to handle alone. More will be said of this later. The point we should remember here, and when working with a person on a decision problem, is that a decision may create additional problems which must be attended to, some of which may be in the nature of a crisis.

Summary. We've considered five types of problems in living. Each must be approached with certain points in mind. Interpersonal conflicts can be resolved only if both partners to the conflict are involved with the caseworker. Difficulties in role performance result from one or more of the following: (1) inadequate skills; (2) conflicts between the various ways the person and those around her define what is expected in the role performance; and (3) the necessity of performing two competing roles at the same time. Reactive emotional distress will diminish more rapidly when the client not only talks about her feelings with the caseworker but, in addition, does something on her own behalf that involves constructive contact with a person other than the caseworker. Problems of inadequate resources frequently involve multiple tasks for not only the worker and the client but also other persons who may have access to resources. Problems with formal organizations require the worker to be an advocate for the client in a way which generates respect from the other professionals involved. Decision problems are "value dilemmas" for clients whose choices may bring on other problems of a crisis proportion.

Exercise

Look back at the problem you described in Chapter IV. Using the various problem types discussed in this chapter, identify the appropriate problem type _____ . In the following space describe one case you have carried or are carrying which fits each of the other problem types discussed.

Problem Type   Problem Description

_____   _____

                     _____

                     _____

_____   _____

                     _____

CRISIS INTERVENTION

Crisis: an unexpected problem in living.[2] A crisis is a problem in living that comes upon us like a storm—frequently unexpected—and shakes us to the roots, demanding, getting, and
sapping our energy. A crisis is like stepping on an icy sidewalk:
Few people escape being thrown off balance and upset by
events such as the premature birth of a baby, getting married,
becoming a parent, becoming unemployed, being raped, termi-
nal or life threatening illness, getting divorced, attempting suicide, or the death of a family member. Each of these events
generates stress, which is potentially a crisis for the individuals
involved.

A crisis occurs for the person who finds her usual approach
to coping with stressful situations inadequate to the demands of
a special situation. Consider for comparison a person who is
taking a quiet ride in a canoe and who suddenly rounds a bend
in the river to see rocks and rapid water. He immediately begins
to paddle as hard as he can to escape the tug of the current. He
strikes a rock, the canoe turns over, he is thrown into the
current and struggles violently to swim to shore. He will likely
be seriously injured, or drown. He either did not know or in his
panic forgot that in rapid water one must relax and go with the
current until he surfaces downriver from the rapids. His usual

fashion of handling the problem of turning over in his canoe did not work. He panicked, became overwhelmed by the situation, and could not successfully deal with it.

But what if he had had a highly skilled partner in the canoe with him, or nearby on the shore? As the canoe is turning over the partner tells him what actions he can take in order to get through the crisis. "Go with the current, relax, don't fight it!" The crisis becomes a turning point in this person's life. Instead of being overcome with terror and the destructive consequences of defeat, the person comes through the crisis better off than he was before the stressful event. He has imprinted indelibly in his memory his successful handling of the situation, and he has demonstrated the skills to handle it again should it arise. How glad we are that his friend, the expert, resisted the temptation to attempt to rescue him by swimming to him. Both might have drowned. Even if the rescue attempt had been successful, the person would have indelibly imprinted on his memory how inadequate he was and how someone else to whom he will be ever grateful was adequate. What a difference it makes when someone is able to help you help yourself!

That's what crisis intervention is about. The caseworker must have an adequate knowledge of various situations to understand what in those situations poses life crises to persons and what the client is able to do to help herself successfully get through a crisis. The material that follows examines a number of life crises, points up the significant variables in each, and suggests tasks that the client can do to cope more effectively in each instance.

The approach to working with persons in these situations follows the same pattern as previously presented. The difference is that the person will be *very* anxious and tense but will identify the target problem very easily. The caseworker must move immediately to support and encourage the client to reduce her anxiety. Before the first interview is over, she should have explored the various aspects of the problem and how the client has attempted to resolve it. Usually the caseworker's identifying the situation as one that easily overwhelms will relieve the client somewhat. In addition, before the co clusion of the first interview a client task and appropriate tasks for the worker are agreed upon. Crisis intervention usually involves seeing or contacting the client by phone very soon—sometimes the same day, at least in two or three days. No more than four to six interviews are needed in most cases for the client to have things back in balance and moving along well on her own.

Premature birth. The birth of a baby is a stressful event in the life of a family. If the birth is premature, the demand on the mother is significantly higher. First, the mother may feel she has failed. She has failed to carry her baby full term as a mother should. Second, the baby may die or have a physical abnormality. Third, the mother will be temporarily separated from the baby while the baby is kept in the premature nursery. This may be a matter of months in which the mother is at home and the baby is in the hospital. Fourth, she will have an especially difficult task in providing the required specialized care once the baby is at home. Each of these target problems must be dealt with.

The first two problems and a part of the third involve the emotional reaction of the mother (and perhaps the father). If the mother responds openly and directly to the facts as they are, she will express guilt at having not met her responsibility to carry the infant to full term. She will express anxiety over the health of her baby and grief in anticipation of the possible loss of the child. Anger and sadness will also result from the unexpected separation while the infant is kept in the premature nursery. These are appropriate and necessary *tasks* for the mother to accomplish in the first days following the birth. When the mother (and probably the father) reacts as though there is nothing with which to be concerned and is unruffled by the situation, there is cause to be alarmed. This is a massive denial of facts. This mother, too, must accomplish the task of expressing her feelings over her failure, the danger to, and possible loss of, the infant, and the separation brought about by the continued hospitalization of the baby after the mother's release. The *task of the worker* in this regard is to talk openly about the facts, thus gently causing the client to face the reality as it is. This action by the worker breaks through the denial of the mother, causing her to express intense emotions to support her contention that nothing is wrong. The worker must empathically respond to this mother by acknowledging and reflecting the feelings, gently allowing the client full expression of all her emotions, being careful not to cut them short by early support and expressions of hope.

> **Worker:** You know you were not able to carry Tim your full nine months, so he's going to have a hard time for the next six to eight weeks.
>
> **Client** (mild irritation): I don't know why you say that! He's doing just fine!
>
> **Worker:** I wish he was doing just fine, and I know you do, too. But that's just not the case. He's lost another three ounces. He weighs only three pounds now. That's two and one-half pounds less than he would weigh if he had been full term, (all said warmly, quietly, and gently).
>
> **Client** (clearly irritated): I don't know why you keep mentioning "if he were full term," as if it was my fault.
>
> **Worker:** You're pretty upset about that possibility, its being your fault?
>
> **Client** (openly angry): You're mighty right, I'm upset! You've no right to say that! I did everything the doctor told me to do.
>
> **Worker:** You wanted the baby to be full-term, (focusing on the good intentions of the client).
>
> **Client** (tearfully): I wanted so much for him to be strong and healthy. I can't imagine what I did wrong, why I could not carry him.
>
> **Worker:** It's hard to accept that, but it did happen. And you did do everything you could, but it just didn't work out that way. Now we're really going to hope that he makes it through.

The client has been moved from denial of the facts of prematurity to beginning to face the situation. She has acknowledged that somehow she had a part in the early delivery, although she doesn't know what. She will come back to this another time, since there are inevitably things which she did during the pregnancy which she didn't intend to do or considered of limited risk. The worker, by refusing to run from the client's anger or to accuse the client of being insensitive, and by resisting the temptation to rescue the client when she began to express her guilt, has enabled the client to begin to work her way through this crisis. Not to express and to deal with these emotions locks the client in a frightening world of unreality, a world which will get worse rather than better.

Additional tasks must be accomplished by the mother and the worker regarding the problem of extended separation from the baby. The task for the mother is to establish an emotional bond with the baby. This will involve frequent visits to the hospital to spend time with Tim as he is able more and more to be cared for by his mother. The worker's task is to keep the mother aware of Tim's need to see her and to make the hospital visits possible through transportation and other resources. The final task for the mother is to learn how to meet Tim's specialized needs after he returns home. This task will likely be accomplished through her visits to the premature nursery. A member of the nursery staff will have the task of teaching the mother what she needs to know. The worker will have the task of assisting the mother in getting together the necessary infant-care equipment and supplies she may need.

During all of these happenings, the father of the baby may be having similar problems, but problems of a different degree. Effort should be made to engage to face the situation and explore his feelings. Many of the tasks of gathering resources can be handled by him. The mother and father should be given the mutual task of sharing their thoughts and feelings with each other. Thus the crisis may strengthen their relationship against future stresses.

Role changes and loss of status. Lots of situations fall under this category. Always there is a loss of role and a taking up of a new one. Always there is a change in the person's importance (primarily in her own eyes, but sometimes as others see it as well) as a result of the role change. Although most of the time there is a significant loss in status, the opposite can also create a crisis, as when an adolescent not used to being the best student in his class becomes the only one making an A. He thought the A was great; his parents did as well, and his teacher praised him highly. His friends teased him but did not reject him. The big problem now is how to keep on making As. His parents expect it, his teacher says she "knows he can do it," and he is so anxious about tests that he can't sleep for a week before one.

The same situation can occur with new mothers who want to do everything just right with their first child or with persons who move from the ranks of the unemployed to what looks like "the first real opportunity I've ever had." In every situation, whether due to a loss of status or a gain, the role involved has become the *one* way by which the person measures his or her importance. Such was the case of many very wealthy businessmen in the Great Depression of the 1930s who, upon realizing that they had lost all their wealth in the crash of the stock market, jumped from the windows of office buildings in New York, Philadelphia, and other large cities.

Public welfare caseworkers encounter the status losers and the status gainers. The immediate target problem in these situations is the excessive emotional reaction of the client. The task for the client is to express her feelings about the change and to define as clearly as possible how she will carry out the new role to suit her satisfaction. Getting the new role in perspective and accepting the situation as one with which she must live, even if only temporarily, must be accomplished if a setback is to be avoided.

Certainly we do not want a person who suddenly finds herself unemployed to be satisfied with remaining unemployed. But until she accepts that role as a fact, she will not likely make any moves toward finding a job. Accepting something is not necessarily liking it, just acknowledging the reality of it. That is the first task of the client. The second is defining the new role and rehearsing its performance.

The physical characteristics of the client and the caseworker. There are obvious differences in physical characteristics that are best acknowledged by the caseworker and the client together as having some effect on the casework relationship. These are race, age, and sex. As a rule, the caseworker's verbal acknowledgment with the client where there is a difference in any or all of these characteristics communicates to the client that the worker will be sensitive to the unique opinions and feelings of the client which grow out of these differences. This does not mean that there is necessarily an issue to be dealt with; rather, there is a difference to be appreciated, valued and understood.

Other physical differences may not be acknowledged by the worker with the client but need to be taken into account by the worker as the casework relationship is examined during the helping process. The size of a client, particularly a very large client with a very small worker, may have subtle effects on both persons. Large persons may like more physical space. Small persons may feel overwhelmed and frightened by the sheer mass of a large person. The physical handicap of a client may or may not have relevance to the goals for casework services. As a matter of course in examining the impact of the problem on the client, the limitations of the client will be considered. Only if the casework goals indicate a need to do so should the worker examine the impact of the handicap on the casework relationship. It could be that such an examination would be very appropriate. In other cases the goals of services can be more efficiently carried out without such an examination.

Aspects of the client such as retardation, physical illness, mental instability, and emotional instability must be considered under physical characteristics. The mentally retarded client is one who has serious problems in learning and in managing changing social situations. The caseworker needs to bear in mind that this client has a limited vocabulary, doesn't understand many multisyllable words, and talks in sentences rather than in paragraphs. Her knowledge of math will be quite limited. She will have a limited store of information and may well be unable to provide all the data the caseworker may need.

In addition, this client will experience considerable anxiety in new situations. This may show up in awkwardness, low verbal interaction, and uncertainty regarding appropriate behavior. It is appropriate for the caseworker to assist this client in bringing together facts and helping the client to recognize the best course of action. This means that a larger measure of worker influence enters the casework process. In addition, the worker should determine that the client has access to ongoing support from family, friends, or neighbors or, where necessary, from casework in regard to meeting life tasks which require math computation, decisions about major purchases, and long-term planning.

The caseworker should be aware of the chronic medical problems of her clients. Some medical problems have a substantial effect on the personality of the client as well as on the need for additional or unusual support systems. Most physicians are willing to respond to specific questions the caseworker may have regarding a client's condition. The caseworker should provide the physician with a proper release of information, have the questions specifically stated in writing, and suggest that, if the physician is unable to take the time to talk directly to the caseworker, a contact through the nurse by phone would be acceptable. Never expect a written response, although you may expect a physician on occasion to be willing to talk directly with you. Never ask a physician an open-ended question unless you want to lose your next opportunity for a contact. Be specific. "I've noticed Mrs. S is very nervous now and wondered if it is connected with her illness. Are there any medically related needs I should be attending to with her?"

Some clients are mentally unstable. Their problems in personal functioning are not those of intelligence but those of organizing their thoughts and being oriented to their life situations well enough to take care of the typical tasks of everyday living. It is possible for a client to have sufficient losses in recent memory due to disease, anxiety, or depression to be unable to keep ideas orderly, to have recall of information needed, or to be completely oriented to the situation. It is as if the client moves in and out of touch with what's happening around her. In extreme cases the client may be organizing her ideas in a rather bizarre fashion, perhaps believing there is a conspiracy against her. In an extreme case of instability, the client may have paranoid delusions accompanied by hallucinations in which she hears voices or sees things that are not present. Medication is usually effective in such cases. This client should be in regular contact with the mental health center. In the process of casework services, the caseworker should be careful not to argue with the client. Communication should express normal warmth and concern for the well-being of the client while not getting into a discussion with the client regarding her fears in connection with the imagined conspiracy. Discuss with her reality based resource needs, immediate problem-solving tasks, and other matters arising out of daily living. Acknowledge the client's anxiety and encourage her to continue her contact with the mental health center, with you and with her friends in the community (who are probably diminishing in number). Helping this client maintain a support system of friends, neighbors, and family may be the most important part of casework. When a person begins to lose some of her mental functioning, those close enough to observe become anxious and sometimes fearful. Even caseworkers do. Loss of mental functioning is not necessarily a sign of the client's being a risk to anyone other than herself. With the proper medication she will not even be a risk to herself in most cases.

A client who is emotionally unstable is one whose moods seem to swing from highs to lows or from being placid to being agitated and on the edge of loss of control. As a rule, such clients do well on the proper medication. Referral to the mental health center for this medication is necessary. Due to the unexpected changes in this client's emotions, the caseworker should be careful not to put this client in a stressful situation during the interview. Interviews should be kept brief and to the point, though accompanied by the warmth and concern of the worker. Never argue with this client, even if you are certain you are right. Simply state that you would like to be sure about your information and will be certain you have missed nothing. If the client seems to be agitated be sure to give her plenty of breathing room. Sit back in your chair and demonstrate a calm, settled demeanor. If anger seems to be erupting from the client be careful not to move in on her. Stay calm, speak quietly, and *never* reach out and touch her. If you need to leave the room explain your intended actions before moving in order not to surprise the client. Stay in good contact with the client. Interrupt her politely to slow down her distress. "Excuse me for interrupting you but I was wondering if you could repeat what you said a few moments ago. I didn't quite understand." Such calculated interruptions about specific facts the client has described tend to engage the client's cognitive processes and reduce the emotional extremes. Try to control a natural tendency to withdraw or run from this client. The best outcome can be achieved if the caseworker maintains a steady and concerned contact.

In all cases similar to those described above, a major concern of the caseworker is to assist the client in securing appropriate services from other community agencies and in helping her maintain a community support system to meet ongoing needs. If the focus can be maintained in that fashion there should be little problem in keeping the relationship helping and professional.

Exercise

Think about one of your "difficult clients." Note what you consider the possible sources of difficulty to be. Refer to the sources listed in this chapter. As you list the possible sources, state your reasons for drawing your conclusion.

_____

_____

_____

_____

_____

What are your thoughts about how you might deal more effectively with her in the future?

_____

_____

_____

_____

_____

9

TAKING CARE OF YOURSELF

"Burn-out" is a term frequently used to refer to persons in the helping professions who have lost all satisfaction in providing services to people. Their motivation is gone. In its place are fatigue, apathy, and negativism. These persons have burned out because they did not take care of themselves, and because the organization in which they worked did nothing to deal with the stress that comes with people-serving demands. There is much that an organization can do to reduce worker stress and improve worker satisfaction. But my concern is with what the worker can do to take care of herself.

First, build a support system at work. You need two kinds. You need colleagues to whom you can express your frustration, colleagues who will not hold your frustration against you or will not mishear your frustration as complaining. A supervisor or fellow worker can fill this bill well. Another kind of support system which is needed is technical. Know where you can get the information or consultation you need regarding various kinds of client problems. Support persons may be in your agency as well as outside in other agencies. Build a list of support persons and how each may be helpful.

Design your day with a change of pace. Everyone knows that the pace in a public welfare office can become hectic. Nevertheless, be sure you take time out for lunch as well as for a relaxed, no-business break in the morning and the afternoon. Learn how to use these periods for relaxation. In only a few minutes tensed muscles can be relieved by using some of the self-help techniques recently publicized. At the least, you can sit back in your chair, place both feet flat on the floor, let your hands rest in your lap, close your eyes, breathe deeply, and picture in your mind a calm scene—like the ocean, a placid place you've been in the mountains, or a lake or stream. You might try tensing your muscles in your whole body momentarily until you literally shake as you tense them. Then let go, back to the relaxed position with your eyes closed, breathing deeply, perhaps imagining that you can see in your mind's eye your breath as it enters a spot in the center of your forehead, following it as it moves down through every part of your body, finally to the tips of your toes; then as you exhale follow it back up through your body to your forehead. Some people find that they relax more if in addition to imagining a placid scene in their minds they repeat to themselves the word "one" in order to keep any stressful thoughts from distracting them. Five minutes a day of such relaxation will add a new dimension to the life of anyone who will try it. Once in the morning, once in the afternoon, and once in the evening and your stress level will drop substantially.

This may sound like something from an eighth grade course in health, but it's true: exercise and proper diet have a lot to do with keeping your body in shape and keeping your stress level down. If you've not been exercising regularly, it's a good idea to start very slowly and progressively work up to a full or strenuous routine. If you've not had a physical checkup lately, you should have one to be sure you are ready for the fitness program you intend to follow.

Finally, get ready for tomorrow before you leave work today so that you will not have to worry about it tonight. This means at the minimum making out a "do list" of what needs to get done the following day. You may want to get some materials or cases out and in order so that you can move into an organized piece of work as soon as you get to your desk. You'll feel a lot better if, after thirty minutes at work, you have a sense of accomplishment already, rather than a feeling of just getting started and being overwhelmed by what's before you.

Stay in touch with your body. Listen to what it says to you about your level of stress. If you feel tight and worn out you must not be taking care of yourself. For your own sake, as well as for the client who needs you to be at your peak of competence, take care of yourself. Thus, you'll never "burn-out."

Exercise

How do you take care of yourself?
List below:

(1) Regular exercise, what kind and when _____

_____

(2) Relaxation or meditation procedure followed daily; what and when_____

_____

_____

(3) Means of organizing and pacing your day _____

_____

_____

_____

(4) Identify your people support system:
     In your agency _____

_____

_____

Outside your agency _____

_____

_____

How does your agency organize itself to guard its members
from burn-out? _____

_____

What suggestions could you make to your supervisor or adminis-
trator to improve the agency support system? _____

_____

_____

NOTES

1. Unpublished text of comments by an anonymous client.
2. Many of the ideas expressed in this chapter were stimulated by Aguilera and Messick (1978).

REFERENCES

AGUILERA, D. C. and J. M. MESSICK (1978) Crisis Intervention, 3rd. ed. St. Louis: C. V. Mosley.

BENJAMIN, A. (1969) The Helping Interview, 2nd. ed. Boston: Houghton Mifflin.

EGAN, G. (1975) The Skilled Helper. Monterey, CA: Brooks/Cole.

EPSTEIN, L. (1977) Report of the Task-Centered Service project, vol. 1. August.

FISHER, J. (1978) Effective Casework Practice. New York: McGraw-Hill.

GARRETT, A. (1942) Interviewing: Its Principles and methods. New York: Family Service Association of America.

IVEY, A. E. and J. AUTHIER (1978) Microcounseling, 2nd. ed. Springfield, IL: Charles C. Thomas.

KADUSHIN, A. (1972) The Social Work Interview. New York: Columbia University Press.

LIDE, P. (1967) "An experimental study of empathic functioning." Social Service Rev. 41: 23-30.

MANN, J. (1973) Time Limited Psychotherapy. Cambridge, MA: Harvard University Press.

PARAD, H. J. [ed.] (1965) Crisis Intervention. New York: Family Service Association of America.

PERLMAN, H. H. (1979) Relationship: The Heart of Helping People. Chicago: University of Chicago Press.

REID, W. J. (1978) The Task-Centered System. New York: Columbia University Press.

——— and L. EPSTEIN (1972) Task-Centered Casework. New York: Columbia University Press.

RYAN, W. (1976) Blaming the Victim, rev. ed. New York: Vintage.

STEINMETZ, S. K. and M. S. STRAUS [eds.] (1974) Violence in the Family. New York: Harper & Row.

TOWLE, C. (1958) Common Human Needs, rev. ed. New York: National Association of Social Workers.

QUESTIONNAIRE
HELP US DESIGN FUTURE GUIDES FOR YOUR USE

First, about this guide

1. What did you find most useful in the book?

2. Do you think it can be improved in future editions? How?

3. Who do you think it would benefit by reading it, or by using it as part of a more comprehensive training or educational program?

4. Can we quote you? _____ If so, please give us your name _____,
degree_____, position _____.

Now lets look to the future

1. What additional topics or issues would you like us to cover in the Sage Human Service Guide series?

2. Are you or someone you know working on a volume that might fit the series? Please describe. Would you like an "Author's Guide?" To whom should it be sent?

3. Are you interested in exploring the possibilities of purchasing bulk orders of Sage Human Service Guides at substantial

savings for use or resale by your organization? Let us know who to be in contact with.

4. Would you like to meet the author of this or one of the other Guides? Are you interested in exploring the development of workshops for your staff or under your organization to auspice with a group of Sage Human Service Guides authors and associates? Tell us whom to contact.

Address your response to: Armand Lauffer, Ph.D.
                              School of Social Work
                              The University of Michigan
                              Ann Arbor, Michigan 48109
                              (313) 764-9485

ABOUT THE AUTHOR

James A. Pippin, MSW, is an Instructor of Social Work and Director of the Extended MSW Program of the University of Georgia. He is a licensed Marriage and Family Counselor. He is a candidate for the EdD degree in Higher Education at the University of Georgia. Previous publications include: *Casework in Public Social Services, Casework Interviewing Effectiveness* (a video training package, joint author) *Intervention Techniques for Social Service Workers, Working With Difficult Clients [Part I The Disturbed Client, Part II The Angry Client]* (a video training package in two parts, author and joint author).

HV43 .P53   c.1
Pippin, James A. cr.   100106   000
Developing casework skills / J

3 9310 00065799 7
GOSHEN COLLEGE-GOOD LIBRARY

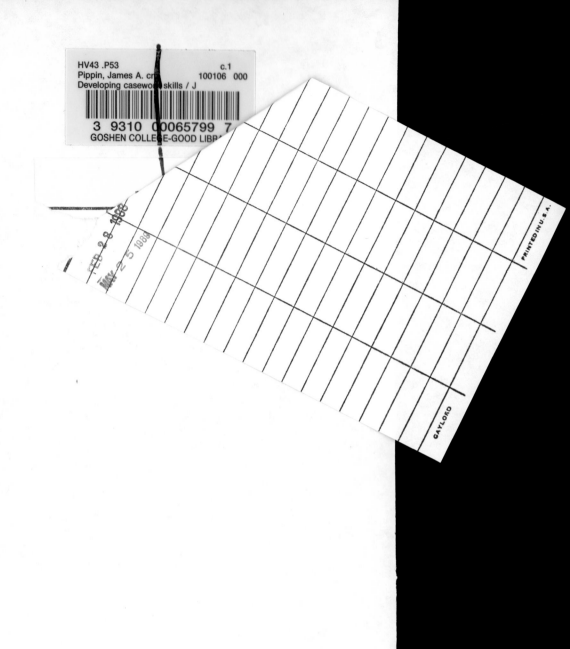

ABOUT THE AUTHOR

James A. Pippin, MSW, is an Instructor of Social Work and Director of the Extended MSW Program of the University of Georgia. He is a licensed Marriage and Family Counselor. He is a candidate for the EdD degree in Higher Education at the University of Georgia. Previous publications include: *Casework in Public Social Services, Casework Interviewing Effectiveness* (a video training package, joint author) *Intervention Techniques for Social Service Workers, Working With Difficult Clients [Part I The Disturbed Client, Part II The Angry Client]* (a video training package in two parts, author and joint author).

HV43 .P53   c.1
Pippin, James A. cr   100106 000
Developing casework skills / J

3 9310 00065799 7
GOSHEN COLLEGE-GOOD LIBRARY

DATE DUE